ROMAN MIDDLEwiCH
A Story of Roman and Briton in Mid-Cheshire

Written by
Tim Strickland

Paintings by
Graham Sumner

Designed by
Chris Bullock

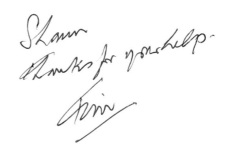

Roman
Middlewich
Piecing the past together

Supported by the
Heritage Lottery Fund

Published by The Roman Middlewich Project
and supported by The Heritage Lottery Fund.

This book is dedicated to all those Roman Army officers and civilian administrators who, largely unsung and unrecorded as always, worked hard and selflessly to bring and maintain the benefits of a lasting and, on the whole, good imperial peace to Britain.

© The Roman Middlewich Project
First published 2001

Printed in GB by Printfine Limited, Liverpool

Published by The Roman Middlewich Project

ISBN 0 9541186 0 X

front cover painting: A Cornovian tribesman and a Roman trooper meet by the river at Middlewich when the Roman Army moved northward through the area, in the search for Caratacus, in AD 48.

FOREWORD

As you will discover from reading this book, many finds have been made in Middlewich over the years, dating from the mid-eighteenth century. We have always felt that the importance of Middlewich in terms of its Roman history has been under-valued, if not neglected. This book and this Project are our opportunity to put the record straight.

As the Project has developed, the scale and the variety of new archaeological evidence has begun to provide an exciting and novel insight into the historical significance of Middlewich.

Now this has been brought together in a way we can all understand and appreciate. Alongside, and informed by the book, we have the new Romans exhibition in the library, a resource pack for use in our local schools, a Roman trail complete with leaflets and interpretation panels, and a group of guides who are trained to take us round the trail.

All these things give us great hope for the future. Now Middlewich is firmly on the map of Roman Britain! However, the completion of this project is only the beginning, and if the discoveries made so far are a pointer to the future, then the continuing story of Roman Middlewich will be an interesting one.

On behalf of the Town Council and the people of Middlewich, I would like to thank the Heritage Lottery Fund for providing the essential funding for the Project. I thank and acknowledge the Project Partners: Cheshire County Council, Congleton Borough Council, Middlewich Heritage Society and Gifford & Partners Ltd. They successfully bid for the funding but more than that, they have produced something important, exciting and of benefit for Middlewich, its residents and its many visitors.

Finally, I would like to thank and congratulate Tim Strickland for this book, which was essentially his brainchild and which is the story of Roman Middlewich we have always wanted.

I am sure you will enjoy this book as much as I have, and share a renewed pride in our town of Middlewich.

Councillor Jacki Cox
Town Mayor

PREFACE

It has been an exciting and stimulating experience assembling and explaining the historical significance of events and developments in the establishment at Middlewich when it was a part [a small part perhaps but clearly a significant one] of Rome's great imperial adventure in Britain during the first four centuries or so AD. To some, it may seem that this is a very familiar story but we should never underestimate its enduring interest to the general public; and, of perhaps greater importance, the lessons and parallels it conveys for us today are perhaps as many and significant as ever they were. With the steady erosion of the place which classical civilization holds in both our national consciousness and educational curricula, and the ever-increasing tendency in our society for historical dumbing-down and revisionism, I wonder sometimes where we will all be if the lessons of history are not learnt and re-learnt at every opportunity. Rome has much to teach us all in this respect. Thus, for me, my involvement in the Roman Middlewich Project, of which the writing of this book has been a major part, has had an interesting and important justification: as a timely reminder of the crucial part which a knowledge of history plays in helping us to understand ourselves.

In assembling all the information and archaeological evidence on which this book is firmly based, I have been constantly surprised at both its quantity and quality. It has, of course, included the reports of eighteenth and nineteenth century antiquarians, the results of the small-scale archaeological research of the 1960s and 1970s, many chance discoveries and even, in recent years, the finds discovered by metal-detectorists which have been reported responsibly and which are now recorded in the County Sites and Monuments Record. Also, in recent years, there have been a number of archaeological surveys and excavations which have resulted, paradoxically, from developer-funded work associated with conditions imposed by the Local Planning Authority. Above all, and perhaps the most outstanding of these, was the discovery [or re-discovery?] in 1993 of the Roman fort at Harbutt's Field. In the event, this became the principal stimulus to the establishment of this project and thus, coincidentally, to the writing of this book. Nonetheless, I hope that this book will be seen only as a beginning and a spur to renewed archaeological and historical research in the Middlewich area. As Councillor Jacki Cox, Mayor of Middlewich Town Council says, this is long overdue. It is a pointer, too, to what can be done, if the will is there, not only at Middlewich but elsewhere as well.

There are so many who have been associated with preparation of this book that it would be impossible to mention them all here by name, but my considerable gratitude is due to them without in any way divesting myself of a personal responsibility for any errors of fact, interpretation or omission which must be mine alone. Many of them are acknowledged more fully at the end of this book. I hope I have remembered them all and my apologies to anyone I have forgotten.

However, as with any good project, this book has been the result of effective teamwork and I would like to record here my considerable debt to the following for their readily-given assistance and support throughout:

Dan Garner, archaeologist with Gifford and Partners, for his sustained and meticulous research and analysis of the archaeological data, for many discussions, revisions and interruptions which have provided the essential basis for this book;

Chris Bullock, for the design of this book, for administering the production and amendment of the illustrations, and for organising the printing of the book.

Shawn Stipling, of Aquarium Graphic Design, for patiently coping with requests for corrections to the proofs at short notice.

Claire Duval, for much support, administrative assistance, typing and re-typing;

Gill Reaney, CAD technician at Giffords, for the finds maps and interpretation plans;

Graham Sumner, for the paintings and many of the cameo illustrations in the book;

My fellow-members of the Roman Middlewich Project's Steering-Group:
Adrian Tindall, (Chairman), Principal Archaeologist, Cheshire County Council
Harry Hopkinson, (Vice-Chairman), Conservation & Design Manager, Congleton Borough Council
Jonathan Williams, (Secretary), Town Clerk, Middlewich Town Council
Gwyneth Jones, Heritage and Museums Officer, Cheshire County Council
Jane Weir, Middlewich Heritage Society
Ruth Goodfellow, Policy & Marketing Officer, Congleton Borough Council
Malcolm Thurston, Local Roman Historian and Poet
Peter Cox, Volunteer and Environmental Warden for Middlewich Town Council;
for sustained advice, support and friendship;

and last, but by no means least, the Heritage Lottery Fund for providing the major part of the funding which has made it all possible.

TIM STRICKLAND

CONTENTS

INTRODUCTION

Stray finds and other chance discoveries relating to the Roman establishment at Middlewich have been made, usually as a result of major new construction works such as those for the turnpike, canal, railway and property development, for over two hundred and fifty years. The earliest surviving record of them is in the form of a letter from Ralph Vernon of Warmingham dated 15 May 1750. In it he says that:

'...I never had an opportunity to make a thorough search for CONDATE [the Roman settlement] but since I have, and am very certain I have found it, for... about half a mile from Middlewich [Kinderton area], and close to the Roman Way [King Street], there is as regular a Roman camp as any in England...'

Learned discussion continued amongst antiquarians in the years that followed, much of it concerning the discovery of the supposed Roman camp at 'Harbutt's Field' [Harbutt's Field in those days appears to have extended much further south]. A hundred years later, in 1850, and after carrying out what we today would call soundings, Archdeacon Isaac Wood proposed to Chester Archaeological Society that:

'Kinderton, near Middlewich, will, I think, prove beyond doubt the ancient CONDATE. There is at Kinderton a Roman camp, in what is called 'the Harboro' Field; it is an irregular feature, not a true parallelogram... The fosse is plainly discernible, though it has been greatly defaced by being partially levelled a few years ago...'

1 *(above)*: The location of Middlewich in northwestern England. Note the location of the town in relation to the M6 motorway, the modern counterpart of the Roman road which once headed for the North via Middlewich and the Mersey crossing at Warrington.

Whatever these surface features, which the Archdeacon described as the 'fosse', had been, they had already, by the 1840s, been significantly reduced in levelling of the site. It is clear that they were no longer visible to Thompson Watkin when he published his remarkable book 'Roman Cheshire' in 1886. Watkin, himself, was more careful and circumspect in his search for and identification of the Roman site. Thus:

'The Harbutt's Field, now divided into two... which certainly embraces the greatest portion of the station, has not been explored, with the exception of the small patches... and these have not been dug to any depth. It is evidently chiefly the suburbs, that have been touched by digging...'

Clearly, Watkin had suspected what we now know; that the northern part of the site, what is known today as Harbutt's Field, might contain the focus of the Roman establishment. He goes on to explain, in his usual careful manner, that the 'fosse' features were streams and not defensive ditches. This, also, we now know to have been the case.

Meanwhile, the Vawdrey family, who had lived nearby at Kinderton for many years had, in the way such families do, been gathering artefacts from and developing their own theories about the Roman settlement. Watkin refers to them and illustrates them copiously in his book. Amongst them, the Vawdreys had noted many finds ranging from those recovered during the cutting of the Trent-Mersey Canal, construction of the railway, the building of the town gasworks and many others. Benjamin Vawdrey moved from Kinderton to Tushingham Hall, near Whitchurch, in 1866, and a selection of the better and more complete Roman artefacts from Middlewich went

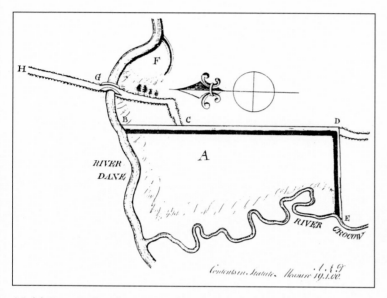

2 Ralph Vernon's plan of the presumed Roman camp at Middlewich dated 1774. The defences, which were described as a 'fosse', are emphasised at B, C, D and E but, as is now clear, the defences of the newly discovered Roman fort in Harbutt's Field lie approximately between the letter A and the River Dane. G H marks the line of the Roman road known today as King Street. Vernon also considered that an 'entrenchment' at F might have been a Roman earthwork.

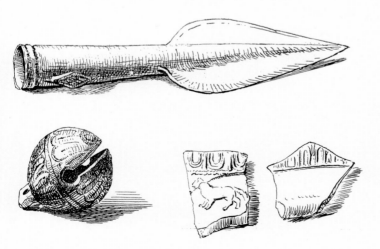

3 Drawings by Archdeacon Isaac Wood of a Roman spearhead, copper bell and fragments of Samian-ware found by him in his soundings near King Street in 1849.

there with him. They remain at Tushingham, where his descendant, Peter Moore-Dutton, displays them proudly to this day.

The Roman roads thought to converge on Middlewich have also been the subject of much debate and speculation for many years. Watkin commented on what, to him, seemed to be a large number [no less than nine were postulated on a map] which suggested to him that the Roman settlement at Middlewich might be second only in importance to the great legionary base at Chester. On the other hand, Archdeacon Wood had earlier drawn attention only to those which we would identify today with confidence: the Chester road, the Nantwich–Whitchurch road, the Chesterton–Warrington road [King Street]. I D Margary, in his renowned and definitive study 'Roman roads in Britain' [Final edition 1973] makes clear reference only to the King Street–Chesterton road (Road 70A) and the Manchester–Whitchurch road (Road 700), both of which, he explains, crossed somewhere in the Middlewich area. On his key-map he also refers to a road heading direct from Middlewich for Manchester. Identifying the exact lines, junctions and crossings of these roads in Middlewich has been and remains notoriously difficult. Although plausible stretches of them have been recorded over the centuries they have been obscured by the development of the town centre. Nonetheless, it is clear that several important roads, and perhaps also some minor ones, did converge on the Roman settlement. Watkin was probably right, after all.

But, perhaps because they are interesting to so many people, the search for Roman roads exemplifies a difficulty in the interpretation of inconclusive archaeological evidence. This is especially true where published accounts have not made sufficiently clear the sometimes subtle distinctions between what is certain and what is possible. Stories abound and 'gather moss' as a result; and soon become a trap for the unwary! Archaeological finds and interpretation relating to the Roman settlement at Middlewich are equally susceptible to such misunderstanding; and great care has been taken throughout this book to restrict the statements made to those for which there is a sound basis in archaeological evidence. The lists of finds and maps will help to demonstrate this.

Another difficulty, hotly debated for centuries, concerns the Roman name for Middlewich. Despite a growing consensus amongst scholars [for SALINAE], the identification will remain unresolved until more conclusive evidence comes to light. One option, listed in the Antonine Itinerary, a Roman route-map probably dating in its original form to the later second or early third centuries, is CONDATE ['Place at the confluence of the rivers']. The other is SALINAE ['saltworks'],

which appears, with CONDATE, in the seventh century Ravenna Cosmography. Either or both would suit Middlewich well but, for the former at least, there is a strong contender in Northwich. The problem arises from the sometimes curious routes selected in the Itinerary. On one interpretation, Northwich seems the more logical as CONDATE since it is mid-way on the direct route (ITER II) from Manchester to Chester. But if, for some reason unclear to us today, the direct route form Manchester to Whitchurch (ITER X) is selected, CONDATE falls mid-way between them; thus indicating Middlewich. Another difficulty arises from the possibility that both Chesterton and Whitchurch may have been called MEDIOLANUM ['Place in the middle of the plain']. Inevitably, this has also led to some confusion in relation to the distances between places on which modern interpretation of the Roman route-maps depends. Furthermore, when the Ravenna Cosmography refers to 'SALINAE' it may not be listing a particular place at all, so much as a region of 'saltings'; in other words Central Cheshire, within which the brine-springs of Northwich, Middlewich and Nantwich lay. Last, many people have noted the striking resemblance of CONDATE to the English placenames 'Kinderton' and 'Kind Street' [nowadays King Street] which coincide closely with the area in which Roman discoveries have been most concentrated at Middlewich. Could 'Kinderton' and 'Kind' thus be derived from CONDATE?

Interest in the true nature of the Roman settlement at Middlewich revived after the First World War, when Professor Donald Atkinson excavated in the area adjacent to the gasworks. There he found extensive traces of Roman ironworking and also, coincidentally, concluded that the defences, which had been described by many before him, had never existed in that area.

4 *(above left)*: Benjamin Llewelyn Vawdrey (1809–1892), a Middlewich Solicitor, recorded many archaeological finds in the area. He moved from Kinderton to Tushingham Hall, near Whitchurch, in 1866. Some of the Roman objects found by him at Middlewich are now at Tushingham.

5 & 6 *(below left and centre)*: Roman flagons made in the second century A.D. found by Benjamin Vawdrey at Middlewich between 1820 and 1866. Now at Tushingham Hall.

7 *(below right)*: Early second century cremation-urn found near Kinderton Old Hall before 1820 and later owned by Benjamin Vawdrey.

One of the most important Roman finds was made accidentally during the building of houses on King Street in 1939. This was a leaf of a bronze discharge diploma issued in AD 105. to a trooper in a regiment of the Roman Army stationed in Britain and known as the ALA CLASSIANA CIVIUM ROMANORUM. Its implications are important for the town because they provide details of an individual who, on retirement and receipt of Roman citizenship, appears to have settled down at Middlewich where he may have been associated with the saltworks.

Further small scale archaeological excavations were carried out off King Street during the early 1960s, all of them revealing features of the Roman settlement. From 1964 to 1975 John Bestwick's excavations to the west of King Street became the largest and most informative ever conducted in the town at that time. They revealed the most extensive and explicit evidence of the Roman saltworks but, although many of the artefacts eventually found their way to the County Council's archaeological collections, little more than brief interim statements and

newsletter articles on these important discoveries has ever been published. Fortunately, however, the artefacts remained available for future study and Mr D A Stubbs, formerly Engineer and Surveyor to Middlewich Urban District Council, himself an active participant in the Bestwick excavations in addition to his own interventions around the town, has been able to provide useful information.

From 1990, the application of the policies encouraged by *Planning Policy Guidance Note 16: Archaeology and Planning* has led to a considerable amount of professionally-conducted archaeological work, ranging from surveys to formal excavation prior to property development. This measure has been so effective that in the last few years no fewer than twenty-eight projects within the Roman settlement have been funded – with the consequent accumulation of a considerable amount of new information, most of it the result of formally conducted work rather than from chance or accidental discovery. Not that the important results of the latter should in any way be underestimated. The Middlewich Heritage Society has bravely kept the

8 *(left):* The commencement of John Bestwick's archaeological excavations at Poolhead Farm in 1972. Note the junction of King Street with Kinderton Street beyond. (John Bestwick is third from the left, at rear).

9 *(above):* Group of Roman Samian-ware cups and bowls discovered during John Bestwick's excavations off King Street, 1964–1975.

banner of archaeological interest aloft over a number of years in which it must have seemed to them that they had been abandoned by officialdom. And, more recently, local metal-detectorists have meticulously and responsibly provided information on their own discoveries.

Important as all this is, perhaps the most outstanding and, in retrospect, significant discovery has been the long-awaited location of the Roman fort in Harbutt's Field in 1993. This, more than any other single event, has provided the stimulus for the currently renewed interest in Roman Middlewich. Two things have arisen from this. First, it has become clear that there is a first-rate story to tell, supported by a surprising wealth of archaeological evidence. Second, that the outcome of archaeological endeavour sustained over no less than a quarter of a millennium could be assembled and interpreted in the light of modern historical understanding. Futhermore, this could at last be done in terms understandable to the general public and to the people of Middlewich, who have for so long wanted to know about their town's Roman origins.

10 A geophysical survey of Harbutt's Field was carried out in 1993. This plot, derived from the survey-readings, provided the first conclusive evidence of the existence of a Roman fort at Middlewich. The defensive ditches and gateways show up particularly clearly.

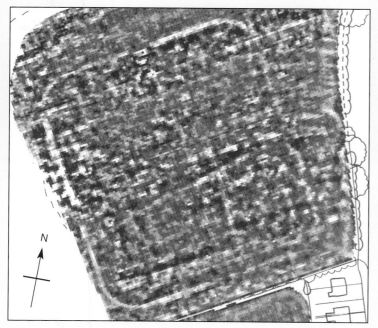

11 *(top):* Excavation prior to proposed development in Harbutt's Field in 1993 revealed this section across one of the defensive ditches of the newly discovered Roman fort.

12 *(above):* Traces of the foundation-trench for a timber-framed wall in a building close to the centre of the Roman fort in Harbutt's Field, 1993.

13 *(left):* Excavation of a second – third century road-surface in the eastern part of the saltworks at Kinderton Hall Farm site in 1999.

14 The people associated with Roman Middlewich: Cornovians, Roman governors, generals, soldiers and their families; saltworkers; early Christian prelates; Anglo-Saxons; eighteenth and nineteenth century antiquarians. *[Painting based on The Altar of Domitius Ahenobarbus].*

ROMAN MIDDLEWICH

A Story of Roman and Briton in Mid-Cheshire

I
BEFORE
THE ROMANS

This chapter describes Middlewich in the Late Iron Age, shortly before the first elements of the Roman Army arrived in the area in the middle of the first century AD. At this date the region was in the northern territory of the Celtic tribe of the Cornovii. Despite the scarcity of evidence for this period from the region as a whole, a surprising quantity of historically significant and explicit archaeological evidence for this period has been recovered from the Middlewich area. A clear picture, which is based closely on this evidence, is built up to show what life was like in the last few years before and at the time of the coming of Rome.

15 *(above)*: In the early first century AD, Cornovian Cheshire was a much less well-drained and watery place across which travel was not always easy. There were numerous marshy soft-spots to be avoided, and the rivers were lined with dense thickets. Although the ancient deciduous forests had been declining for centuries, the open farmland and pastures were still edged with extensive woodland and dense forests. This photograph gives an idea of this environment.

16 *(below)*: It is impossible today to identify the exact limits of the Celtic tribal territories in the region but ancient writers and, occasionally, archaeology have made it possible to piece together and locate the heartlands of the main pre-Roman confederations. This map shows the general locations of the tribes in the region shortly before the Romans moved into it.

I n the early first century AD, Cheshire fell within the northern territory of the tribe of the *Cornovii*. These people tell us nothing of themselves, and our earliest explicit – Roman – references to them are coloured, inevitably, by Roman perspectives. But although the archaeological evidence remains fairly slight, new and more objective historical interpretation has been made possible by a wealth of archaeological, anthropological and ethnographic discovery and related research in recent years from elsewhere in Britain and by reasonable analogy with other tribal societies.

Thus, we may be confident that the *Cornovii* were essentially a Celtic people, speaking a language from which Gaelic and modern Welsh are derived. Nonetheless, although they had been here for at least several hundred years before the coming of Rome, they themselves – driven by those behind them and ever on the lookout for new pastures and new opportunities – must once have moved northward and westward onto land which had belonged to those who had occupied it before them. So, it is not strictly accurate to describe the *Cornovii* as an indigenous people, although they must have long since mixed in with those already here and, no doubt, considered themselves as those to whom the region had always belonged.

The *Cornovii* would also have distinguished themselves readily from the peoples of the tribes around them: the *Ordovices* and *Deceangli* across the River Severn and the middle reaches of the River Dee to the west; the *Dobunni* in modern Worcestershire and Gloucestershire to the south; the *Corieltauvi* [until recently known as the *Coritani*] and perhaps also the powerful and expansive *Catuvellauni* in Warwickshire and Leicestershire to the east and south-east. To the north, across the River Mersey, and also in the Derbyshire Peaks to the north-east, lay the *Brigantes*, a great tribal federation which included sub-tribes such as the *Setantii* in Lancashire, and whose territories stretched northwards even as far as Cumbria and the borders of Scotland.

Although the exact tribal boundaries are notoriously difficult to identify, *Cornovian* territory [the name may be derived from worship of the Celtic horned god *Cernunnos*

17 *(right)*: Late pre-Roman burnished jar and bowl. Fragments of this handmade pottery, which was manufactured in the Malvern area, have been found off King Street, Middlewich. Such pottery was clearly still in use in the area in the first century AD.

and may give a hint of tribal religious allegiances] appears to have encompassed most of modern Cheshire and Shropshire, with parts of Staffordshire and Worcestershire. We can be certain that the *Cornovii* knew where the inter-tribal zones and disputed territories were, and when they crossed uninvited into the lands of other tribes: with all the attendant risks –such as the shouted exchange between hunting parties, or the sudden blow of the knobkerrie, the 'swish' of a spear, or the 'thunk' of an arrow into the tree beside them! Many things would have informed them: a cairn or long-abandoned barrow perhaps, or a particular woodland, a bend in a river, a convenient crossing-point, a decent bit of farmland, a mode of dress, a distinctive tattoo, familiar custom and practice, or perhaps even a dialect. And so, in striving to understand and visualise life in Cheshire before the Romans we need to remind ourselves constantly that this was a world in which the tribe, and loyalty to it or one's part of it, was everything. There was no nationalism and little sense of 'Britishness'. These were concepts which Roman historians, themselves remote from tribalism and an understanding of tribal ways, assigned to them, incorrectly.

Despite the limitations on our understanding, recent research is helping us to build up a picture, and it is interesting to imagine what life was like in the Middlewich area in the early first century AD. As we have seen, people's interests and instincts were dominated

18 *(right):* Reconstruction of a Cornovian sword and bronze scabbard based on complete types found in Yorkshire. The chape from the Middlewich example is illustrated on the end of the scabbard.

19 *(below):* Late pre-Roman bronze scabbard-chape, with red enamel inlay, found near Harbutt's Field. Such finds indicate the presence of a sophisticated Cornovian tribal community in the area before the Romans arrived.

KEY

  Fenland

  Cleared Heathland

  Open Woodland (mixed deciduous)

  Dense Woodland (mixed deciduous)

  Possible pre-Roman Tracks

  Rivers and streams

  Farmstead

  Field-system

  Ford

  Salt marsh/brine springs

Cornovian Middlewich in the Late Iron Age, shortly before the Romans arrived. This interpretation is based closely on archaeological discoveries. The nature and extent of the open ground, agriculture, the mixed deciduous woodland and surviving remnants of the great ancient forests are based on palaeoenvironmental research from Middlewich and from elsewhere in Cheshire.

20 Corieltauvian gold coin found at Warmingham, near Middlewich. Such coins were still circulating in the region, perhaps as payment for salt, in the middle of the first century AD.

21 A Cornovian warrior and his wife at Middlewich, at about the time the Romans moved into the area. The Cornovii were already extracting salt from the local brine-springs.

22 *(right):* Roman tombstone of VEDICA, the only known Cornovian woman, from Ilkley, Yorkshire.

by the tribe, although it is possible that this part of Cheshire, though *Cornovian*, was in fact the heartland of an as yet unknown sub-grouping, or sept, of the greater tribal unit.

We may also assume that among the *Cornovii* there was little experience, still less conception, of the idea of private ownership of property beyond, that is, the chattels of the immediate farmstead or family-group; and, of course, the inevitable personal weapons associated with the coming-of-age of the menfolk, and jealously looked after and sported by them as symbols of manhood. All else – and particularly the land and its more important natural resources – belonged, in common, to the tribe: or, in other words, what was done with it was determined by the chief, or king, and the representatives of his immediate family.

At the head of this society, and gathered about the person of the king, or chief, or lesser chieftains, was a warrior caste – or aristocracy – who by the first century AD appear to have abandoned the great hillforts of the Mid-Cheshire Ridge [Bickerton, Beeston, Eddisbury], where once they had been established, and to have moved down into the adjacent lowlands.

The position of women in the tribe can, on the whole, be described as dependent on the whims of their menfolk –at least in public. But we should be careful not to assume that this necessarily gave women a kind of second class status. Tribal society is not as simple as that: and besides, in first century Britain, some of the greatest tribes of all could be ruled openly by women: queens like *Boudica* [formerly *Boadicea*] of the *Iceni*, and *Cartimandua* of the *Brigantes*. Such women had very considerable status and power over the tribal warriors they ruled, even in open war. *Boudica*, as a case in point, nearly succeeded in destroying the fledgling Roman province of *Britannia* in AD 60!

In times of peace, most of the tribe engaged in what we would recognise today as subsistence farming. Very few people travelled much outside their immediate neighbourhood. The notable exceptions were the priests [perhaps considered sacred holy men, many of them also secure as sons of the tribal aristocracy] and representatives of the trading fraternity who, alone, passed unscathed with relative freedom between the tribes.

Although the native mixed-deciduous woodland remained extensive – and there were still tracts of densely forested country on the heavier soils – the great ancient deciduous forests had already been declining for centuries, with a consequent increase of shrubland, heath and grassland. This long decline of the forests may have been due originally to changing climatic conditions some centuries previously, but it was also the inevitable consequence of steady population growth and an increase in widespread farming-activity. On the other hand, the climate had been improving since the second century BC and this may have further stimulated the farming development. Throughout this lowland landscape, living in scattered settlements and enclosed farmsteads of thatched-roofed round-houses on the lighter and better-drained soils, *Cornovian* farming communities were engaging increasingly in cereal-production: emmer, spelt and bread-wheat, rye and some oats being grown.

On the open grasslands, heathland and hills pastoral farming was extensive. There, a common sight would have been the shepherd leading flocks of sheep and goat, perhaps also herds of small brown cattle. Pigs, reared nearer the settlements and on the farms, scratched for roots and nuts in the adjacent lighter woodlands. We may also imagine extensive foraging, in particular for fruit and nuts and no doubt also for certain plants and herbs. But, over all, there were still the inevitable localised loyalties and attendant differences in outlook: hillfolk *versus* plainsfolk, forest-dweller *versus* farmer. We have these still. Everyone hunted 'for the pot', for this entire landscape was teeming in wildlife –including bear, deer of various types, wolves and very edible wild boar [this last also made for great sport] and, of course, many birds. The rivers were full of fish.

As we have seen, communication for most people was very localised and, to a considerable degree influenced, on the one hand, by farming needs and, on the other, by the sheer difficulty involved in any longer-distance travel, not to mention the small need for it. We forget these difficulties today, surrounded as we are by a highly organised landscape which is the product of centuries of development, improvement and maintenance. In the early first century AD, *Cornovian* Cheshire was, above all, a much less well drained and watery place: there were extensive marshy soft-spots [some of them very dangerous] to be carefully avoided; and the rivers, even the larger streams, still in a wild state, were always relatively difficult to cross, edged as they usually were by more or less impenetrable thickets of fen, reeds and brambles, not to mention squelchy and muddy quagmires. The rare exceptions were the natural fords and crossing-points, where the rivers and streams flowed across the sandstone bedrock or glacial deposits of gravel.

In such a landscape, the crossing-points, offering a rare convenience to the traveller, must have become valuable, even politically important in some cases, very early on and, inevitably, they came to be well used. Thus, the fords across the River Dane [King Street] and River Croco [Kinderton Street] in the Middlewich area were of the greatest importance to the local tribespeople, who were living then, as we now know, in round-houses on the lighter and better-drained land between the two, in what is now the area of King Street. In one sense, therefore, these fords had already become one of the principal locating-factors, or *raisons d'etre*, in the pre-Roman tribal development of what one day would become Middlewich. In the same way, a number of tracks – some of them the beginnings of the main roads which converge on the town today – must also have originated.

23 Ostorius Scapula, distinguished general and governor of the fledgling Roman Province of Britannia from AD 47–52, in dress uniform. Scapula pursued the defeated British war-leader, Caratacus, into Brigantian territory across the River Mersey.

24 Elements of the Roman Army moved northward through central Cheshire in the summer of AD 48, in their search for the British war-leader, Caratacus. In this scene, a Cornovian chieftain meets a Roman trooper by the River Croco at Middlewich. Note the Roman tented marching-camp in the background.

25 Another interesting and unusual later pre-Roman find from Middlewich is this bronze terret-ring which is thought to have come from a chariot-harness.

Amongst those who used the fords were the traders. We have seen already how they were able to travel between the tribes with some degree of freedom. The transactions which they engaged in [sometimes, no doubt, on behalf of kings or chiefs], could be politically important, prestigious even, and often with long-distance travel implications. Perhaps this was the origin and stimulus in the development of some of the more important *Cornovian* trackways. Indeed, some of them elsewhere in Cheshire were already very ancient, and are now known to have been even well over fifteen hundred years old by the first century AD. It seems likely therefore that the road now known as King Street began this way, for it ultimately connected the area, no doubt originally via a series of shorter stretches between settlements and farmsteads, with the *Corieltauvi*, *Catuvellauni* and *Dobunni* to the south and south-east, and the *Setantii* and *Brigantes* to the north and north-east. Furthermore, it was a route which also led the long-distance traveller to the *Cornovian* heartlands in today's central Shropshire on the one hand, on the other to the area of the lowest reasonably convenient natural fording-point across the River Mersey [Warrington]. In addition to this major north-south route, there must have been others; and it seems reasonable to hazard a guess at the existence of an east-west one which might have served as a means of similar communication, via the Middlewich fords, between the *Deceangli* of North Wales and the southern *Brigantes* in the Pennines.

That there was long-distance trade across the region, before Roman times, is well attested by the widespread distribution out of and into the area of certain types of cooking-pot and storage-jar; by the as yet, not fully understood occurrence of Carthaginian and Greek coins at Meols, in the Wirral [surely, evidence of contact with the Mediterranean world in the last three centuries BC]; and, perhaps of even greater significance for our understanding of life at this date in central Cheshire, the rare appearance of *Corieltauvian* gold coins, one of which has even been found at Warmingham, near Middlewich.

Such coins point to large-scale inter-tribal transactions in important commodities –among them hunting-dogs, furs and skins, corn, slaves, copper [mined in the Alderley Edge area for some 1800 years already], iron, gold and silver, weapons of various kinds [some of them beautifully crafted and highly prized]…and salt. This last-named commodity, the salt extracted from the naturally occurring brine-springs of central Cheshire –among them, those at Middlewich – had always been considered essential and much sought-after. Its availability would early have given the area a reputation, both among the *Cornovii* and the adjacent tribes, and also with the traders who transported it – sometimes in earthenware containers but perhaps more usually in sacks or even baskets throughout the region.

Into this tribal world, shortly before the middle of the first century AD, came the first elements of the Roman Army.

26 *(right):* Middlewich in the early first century AD. The site is framed by the Rivers Croco and Dane to the west and north, and a minor stream [once thought to have been a Roman defensive 'fosse' by eighteenth and nineteenth century antiquarians] flows due west across the centre of the picture. A number of pre-Roman trackways, some of them already ancient, converge on the crossing-point in the foreground. There are a number of Cornovian farmsteads on the better-drained, lighter soils in what is now the King Street area, and a hint of some salt-extraction from the brine-springs a short distance to the east. Note that, although there is already extensive open ground and grazing pasture, the area is still surrounded by woodland and remnants of the great primeval deciduous forests.

II
THE ROMAN ARMY AT MIDDLEWICH

27 *(above)*: The Emperor Claudius who ruled AD 41–54. He initiated and presided over the successful invasion of southern Britain in 43. In the later years of his reign the Roman Army arrived in the Middlewich area.

28 *(below)*: The military situation in northwest Britain during the AD 50s .

Independent British

Area of Campaigns AD 47–69

Under Roman Control

MANCHESTER
Seteia
WILDERSPOOL
CHESTER ● NORTHWICH
● MIDDLEWICH
Deva
CHESTERTON
WHITCHURCH
Sabrina
WROXETER WALL

In Part One, the arrival of units of the Roman Army at Middlewich is explained and described. After the successful landings in southern Britain in AD 43, the Emperor Claudius had had great hopes of a speedy and successful conclusion to the advance into the Midlands. But the war-leader, Caratacus, fled to the Silures and Ordovices in Wales and, in so doing, led these tribes into furious guerrilla action against Rome. This resulted in several years of bitter and inconclusive fighting but, eventually, Caratacus was defeated and handed over to Rome. The associated campaigning from 48 to 58 drew the Romans into the territory of the Cornovii and ultimately, via the Middlewich area, to the River Mersey and the Brigantes to the north. In 60, Boudica's Revolt nearly spelt the end of the Roman province. This was followed by a few years of cautious retrenchment and then, in 68, the Emperor Nero's death took the entire Roman World into civil war.

PART ONE: ARRIVAL AD 48–68

In the summer of AD 43 southeastern England became the Roman Province of *Britannia*, but early hopes of a rapid conquest of the rest of the island had been dashed by the *Catuvellaunian* prince, Caratacus. His flight to the *Silures* in what is now south-eastern Wales engaged the Roman Army in a long guerrilla campaign in the West Midlands, Central and North Wales. The pursuit of Caratacus drew the Romans north-westward and elements of the Roman Army were soon established in the lands of the friendly *Cornovii*. But when Aulus Plautius, the general who had led the successful invasion of 43, left for Rome in 47, the tribes beyond the middle reaches of the River Severn remained unsettled.

Ostorius Scapula, the incoming governor, arrived with clear ideas about the need for imposing a firm and decisive military solution on a situation which, he considered, had been festering unresolved for too long. His first tactic of disarming the tribes in the rear – even those who had already been allies of Rome for some years – went down badly and led to a major insurrection which had to be put down before further northward advance was possible. At the beginning of the summer of 48 Scapula felt himself ready to return to the front at last.

To achieve their objective – the final destruction of Caratacus – the Romans mounted a campaign across the Severn into Central and North Wales. This included a move against the *Deceangli* (in Northeast Wales), and it is in this context that we can imagine various units of the Roman Army also active in Cheshire. There, the soldiers had three tasks: first, to act as a screen to the main Roman force which had moved directly against Caratacus, now with the *Ordovices* in Central and Northwest Wales; second, to prevent any anti-Roman disaffection spreading among the *Cornovii*; and third, to provide a show of force in support of Queen Cartimandua, the paramount ruler of the *Brigantes*, who was under pressure from some of her own people to switch allegiance to Caratacus.

Thus, the Roman cavalry units ranged far and wide through the northern territory of the *Cornovii*; often assisted by tribesmen acting as scouts. The Roman soldiers became a familiar sight in the region and, we must remind ourselves, probably, on the whole, a popular one for those *Cornovians* who found peace and the new wealth to be acquired from barter with the troops preferable to the war-option offered by Caratacus.

However, it was the need to support their ally, Queen Cartimandua, which led the Romans northward to the lowest convenient crossing-point of the River Mersey, in the

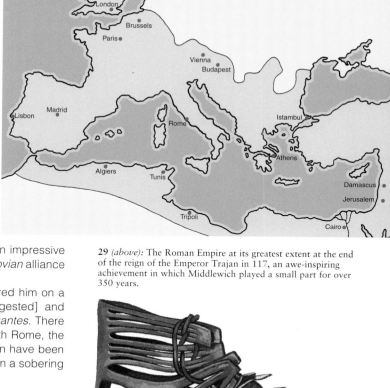

Wilderspool-Warrington area. This single fact meant that the people of the Middlewich area saw Roman soldiers on a very regular basis from then on; for the place was on both of the direct routes northward from the already well-established bases in the Wall (LETOCETUM) and Wroxeter (VIROCONIUM) areas. Both these routes, probably already upgraded by the army into all-weather military roads, converge on Middlewich, one via Whitchurch and the other Chesterton. Of even greater significance, after converging on one or other of the River Croco crossing-points at Middlewich, the Whitchurch and Chesterton roads joined the new main road (King Street) which then headed directly for the Mersey at Warrington. As they passed through, the Roman soldiers must have been an impressive sight. But they were also a reminder and a warning that maintaining the *Cornovian* alliance with Rome would be the wisest course of action.

The fighting against Caratacus continued until Scapula eventually cornered him on a hilltop somewhere near the Upper Severn [Llanymynech has been suggested] and defeated him in pitched battle. Caratacus fled to his friends among the *Brigantes*. There he fell into Cartimandua's clutches and, anxious to preserve her alliance with Rome, the queen handed him over to the Romans. The defeated chieftain may well then have been taken south and hence ultimately to Rome, via Middlewich. It would have been a sobering sight for those who had still hoped for independence.

29 *(above):* The Roman Empire at its greatest extent at the end of the reign of the Emperor Trajan in 117, an awe-inspiring achievement in which Middlewich played a small part for over 350 years.

KEY

 Fenland

Cleared Heathland

Open Woodland (mixed deciduous)

Dense Woodland (mixed deciduous)

Roman Roads

Possible pre-Roman Tracks (still in use)

Rivers and streams

Fort

Field-system

Ford

Farmstead

Salt marsh/brine springs

Central Middlewich in the late first century, interpreting discoveries relating to the presence of the Roman Army.

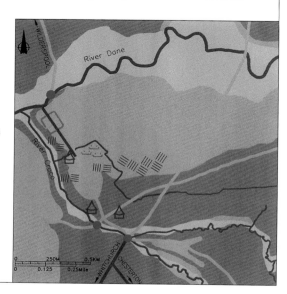

30 & 31 *(above):* Two types of Roman Army footwear: the famous sandal-type caligae [here shown with spur for cavalry use]; and the enclosed boot [also shown with spur] which began to become popular with the soldiers in the first century AD.

32 *(above)*: The Emperor Nero, Claudius's adoptive son, who ruled AD 54–68.

33 *(below)*: From the start of Ostorius Scapula's campaign in 48 to the death of the Emperor Nero in 68, the Roman Army was active in the area on a number of occasions. In this scene a Roman quartermaster barters with a local Cornovian tribesman for salt to be supplied to the soldiers. A fort is under construction at Harbutt's Field in the background.

Despite his ultimate success against Caratacus, Scapula died in 52, worn out by the relentless campaigning, and Didius Gallus hurried to Britain to replace him. Serious fighting continued unabated against the *Silures* and the Romans were not always victorious.

The Emperor Claudius died in 54 and was succeeded by his adoptive son, Nero. There were rumblings of serious trouble in the East, where the Parthians [approximately from modern Iran and Iraq] were exerting political control over Armenia. It was a time for reassessment and caution elsewhere, and the new emperor demanded that Britain be kept quiet. Nonetheless, the continued presence of Roman troops in northern *Cornovian* territory and in *Brigantia* led to further unrest north of the Mersey and in the Pennines, and the legions were moved forward to new bases, in potential support. Thus the Fourteenth Legion (LEGIO XIIII) was established in a new fortress at or close to the tribal centre of the *Cornovii*, at Wroxeter (VIROCONIUM). More than ever before, the people of the Middlewich area then found themselves to be situated on one of the main military arteries to the Mersey. No doubt, too, the place had begun to develop as a convenient halt for Roman units en-route for the North where the presence of such troops was still needed in support of Cartimandua.

Meanwhile, the trouble with the *Silures*, which persisted into the late 50s, was crushed finally by Quintus Veranius who, unfortunately for Rome, died in office before he was able to complete the subjugation of the *Ordovices*. The next governor, Suetonius Paullinus, arrived in 58 with instructions to 'pacify' the *Ordovices* as his top priority.

The pacification of the *Ordovices* led Paullinus into a celebrated campaign against the Druid priesthood on Anglesey. Their imminent suppression may have been connected [the Druids were very influential] with a major uprising amongst the tribes in modern-day East Anglia – well known to all as Boudica's Revolt. In the process, Colchester, London and VERULAMIUM (near St Albans) were burnt to the ground and the province nearly lost. In a lightning campaign, Paullinus marched back across the Midlands to deal with the threat, assembling his forces from units scattered throughout the region, as he went. Soldiers stationed temporarily in forts at Middlewich, Chesterton and Whitchurch may also have been withdrawn to join him. In a classic defensive action, Paullinus destroyed Boudica and her followers in 60.

Seriously worried about the continuing drain on Roman resources, the Emperor Nero came close to abandoning Britain. The situation was made worse by the fact that diplomatic relations with Parthia had broken down into open war, and military distractions elsewhere in the Empire became undesirable and inconvenient. Thus, for the next few years in Britain, a yet more determined policy of consolidation rather than further advance became necessary. And then, in 68, Nero was forced to commit suicide rather than face an infuriated mob in the streets of Rome. The Roman World was plunged into civil war and events in Britain seemed, for a time, unimportant.

34 *(right)*: Roman Middlewich in the middle of the first century AD. A temporary camp is shown in the background and Cornovian farmsteads are scattered across what will one day become the King Street area. Many of the pre-Roman trackways remain in use. A Roman infantry regiment marches from the Chester direction towards the crossing-point on the River Croco, near the site of the bridge which is now at the centre of the town. Note the still extensive woodland and forest.

35 The Emperor Vespasian came out top in the civil war of 68–69. Under him, the policy of total conquest of the British Isles was formulated.

36 Samian-ware bowl found near Ravenscroft Bridge in the 1850s. Such fine tableware was supplied to the Roman Army.

37 Roman Army stew-pot made at Middlewich.

38 Northwest Britain during the early 70s AD. The main routes associated with the campaigns against the Brigantes, and the significance of the Middlewich location on the western route north, heading for the lowest Mersey crossing-point, will be clear.

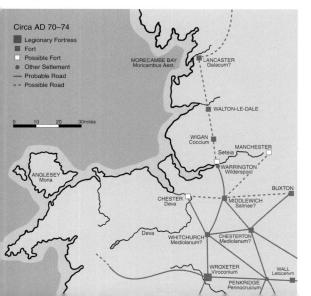

Circa AD 70–74
■ Legionary Fortress
■ Fort
□ Possible Fort
● Other Setlement
— Probable Road
- - Possible Road

0   10   20   30miles

MORECAMBE BAY
Moricambus Aest.
LANCASTER
Galacum?

WALTON-LE-DALE

WIGAN
Coccium
MANCHESTER
Seteia

WARRINGTON
Wilderspool

BUXTON

ANGLESEY
Mona

CHESTER
Deva
MIDDLEWICH
Salinae?

Deva
WHITCHURCH
Mediolanum?
CHESTERTON
Mediolanum?

WROXETER
Viroconium
WALL
Letocetvm

PENKRIDGE
Pennocrucium

After the death of the Emperor Nero in 68 the Roman Empire was plunged into civil war. The anti-Roman faction among the Brigantes saw this as an opportunity and rose in revolt against Queen Cartimandua who was overthrown. A small Roman force failed to restore her to her throne and, under Venutius, the Brigantes abandoned their Roman alliance. An unsettled period followed for the Cornovii. And then, in 69, Vespasian became Emperor. He instigated a forward policy of the total conquest of Britain and Ireland and this was put into effect in the early 70s. The southern Brigantes were suppressed, North Wales pacified and construction of a new legionary base at Chester (Deva) commenced. Events at Middlewich, in the centre of affairs on the main military northward artery west of the Pennines, including the construction of a new permanent auxiliary fort there, are described.

PART TWO: ADVANCE TO THE NORTH AD 69–77

From the death of the Emperor Nero in June 68 to the accession of Vespasian in 69 the entire Roman World was plunged into civil war. This was an uneasy period for the *Cornovii*. Events might easily have gone in either one of two directions: renewed advance by Rome, and hence support for those, like the *Cornovii*, who were allied to her; or withdrawal by Rome leading to reprisals by the disaffected *Brigantes* and *Ordovices* against erstwhile Roman allies. And then, those among the *Brigantes* who had always resisted Cartimandua's alliance with Rome, which seemed to them to be associated with the frequent presence of the hated Roman troops (some of their officers unacceptably close to the queen, as military advisors), noted Rome's pre-occupation with events elsewhere.

They took matters into their own hands. Foremost among them was Cartimandua's consort, Venutius, who had led the Brigantian anti-Rome faction for some years. Relations between him and the queen had broken down several years before, but on that occasion Quintus Veranius had reacted sharply to a perceived threat to a Roman ally, and had sent a legion in.

But in the summer of 68 or spring of 69 Vettius Bolanus, the provincial governor, might not be expected to act decisively. And, to add insult to injury, Cartimandua had even taken the hand of Venutius's former armour-bearer, one Vellocatus, in marriage. Venutius, himself chief of a major sept among the *Brigantes*, could not ignore this slight to his dignity. The continued alliance of his own supporters might be uncertain if he did. The time was right and, when the queen was distracted in an unguarded moment, Venutius managed at last to overthrow her. The queen, of course, immediately sought the assistance of Rome.

Probably to Venutius's surprise, Vettius Bolanus, reacted sharply; but his mixed force of a legionary detachment and some auxiliary cavalry proved insufficient for the purpose. Venutius and his anti-Roman supporters remained in control of the *Brigantes*. A potentially very serious and destabilising force had thus emerged across the Mersey, in northern Britain.

In July 69 the civil war ended with the accession of Titus Flavius Vespasianus, former governor of Judaea. Known to history as Vespasian, the new emperor was not only a highly experienced and successful general but, of great significance for the future of this island, also had extensive firsthand knowledge of Britain. As a young man, he had commanded a legion in the Claudian invasion of 43 and he thus had the knowledge to work out for himself what would be the best actions to take. Little can Venutius and the *Brigantes* have realised what was in store for them!

A new policy, designed to achieve the total conquest of the British Isles, including Ireland, was formulated in 70. The associated campaigning was to be executed with confident and well-supported dispatch. New military units, including the Second *Adiutrix* Legion, were drafted to Britain to assist. Given his own experience of Britain it is no surprise that the next governor appointed by Vespasian was Petillius Cerealis, who also had firsthand knowledge of what would become the main attack-route, east of the Pennines, into *Brigantia*. Vespasian's first instruction to Cerealis must have been 'destroy Venutius and pacify the *Brigantes*'. The Army prepared for action.

West of the Pennines, a major force, consisting of at least one legion and a number of auxiliary regiments, assembled under the young Julius Agricola, commander of the Twentieth Legion, then based at Wroxeter in the old *Cornovian* tribal heartlands. He put in hand a series of major logistical preparations, among them [we may surmise] the checking out and repair or upgrading of all major roads north, the organisation of military supplies, and the construction [or refurbishment] of regimental forts and defended supply-annexes at key locations on the road north. It is probable that the fort at Harbutt's Field, within the confluence of the Rivers Dane and Croco at Middlewich, was built at this time.

Thus, once again, Middlewich found itself on a road well-trodden by the Roman Army. But this time with an important difference: Agricola's was a major force, including the fighting strength of at least one of Rome's crack legions, several thousand men strong. It is interesting to imagine such units passing through and assuming, coincidentally, certain administrative and supply duties over local resources such as the increased production and transportation of salt. The auxiliary cavalry units would also have been very prominent, for they provided the essential screen and scouting-services to the main infantry force. The *Cornovians* living in the neighbourhood would have been very impressed.

As the campaign developed over the next three years or so Middlewich remained a bee-hive of intense military activity, much of it associated with logistical support to the front-lines in northern England. By 74, Venutius had been crushed, and the *Brigantes* – at least the southern septs of this great tribal confederation – cowed for the moment into submission to Rome. It was time to make final preparations for the next steps towards the total conquest of Britain. The Second *Adiutrix* Legion was dispatched to the harbour-mouth of the River Dee and commenced the building of a great new legionary fortress-depot at Chester (DEVA). Next, the final submission of the *Ordovices* in North Wales was to be secured. This was achieved by Julius Frontinus and Julius Agricola over the next three years. In 78 the total conquest of Britain could begin.

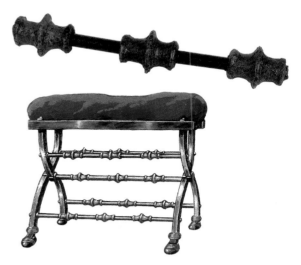

39 *(top)*: Part of a folding camp-stool found in a second century rubbish pit, where it had been discarded, off King Street, 1964–1969.

40 *(above)*: A Roman Army camp-stool. Reconstruction based closely on the piece found at Middlewich.

41 *(right)*: During the Roman campaigns against the Brigantes in the early 70s AD an auxiliary regimental fort existed at Harbutt's Field, and King Street became a major military artery to the North. In this scene, a group of Roman soldiers upgrades King Street, under the watchful eye of a cavalry troop assigned to patrol duties; and in the background loom the defences of the fort.

42 *(above):* The Emperor Domitian, younger son of Vespasian, succeeded his brother, Titus, in 81 and ruled until 96. During his reign troop movements from Britain led to a gradual withdrawal from Scotland.

43 *(below):* Northwestern Britain c.AD 78–c.120. The infrastructure which has developed from the newly built legionary fortress at Chester will be noted; so too will the continuing significance of Middlewich on the main artery, via the Mersey, to the North.

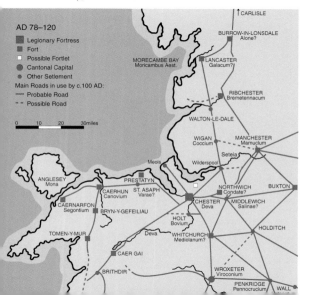

In 78 the Roman Army advanced northward, intent upon the total conquest of the British Isles. By 85 northern Britain was nearly pacified when major warfare, and Roman defeats, on the Danube frontier changed everything. The Emperor Domitian withdrew many army units from Britain and sent them to the Danube. As a result, Scotland had to be abandoned and the Army withdrew southward gradually. By 90 the Twentieth Legion was back at Chester and Middlewich reoccupied by another military unit – possibly the ALA CLASSIANA regiment. The military saltworks continued to develop outside the fort and were under control of the Twentieth Legion. Some soldiers, among them at least one veteran from the ALA CLASSIANA, retired to Middlewich where they may have been involved in saltworking on an entrepreneurial basis. This phase continued until shortly after the accession of the Emperor Hadrian in 117. Within a few years of that, new policies would lead to great changes at Middlewich.

PART THREE: CONQUEST, WITHDRAWAL AND CONSOLIDATION AD 78–C.120

In the Spring of 78 Agricola began to assemble two great military forces, one on each side of the Pennines. Large detachments (*vexillationes*) of no less than four legions provided the hard core: the Second Augustan, the Second *Adiutrix*, the Ninth Spanish and the 'Brave and Victorious' Twentieth. The legions were supported by a large number of auxiliary regiments which ranged from units of specialist troops to infantry, mixed infantry-and-cavalry, to the distinctive cavalry wings (*alae*). They were to be supported, where possible, by the Roman fleet and other legionary detachments – from the Second *Adiutrix* in particular. A major campaign was afoot.

West of the Pennines, the main routes through *Cornovian* territory can be detected : one from Wroxeter via Whitchurch and Middlewich to the Mersey, and then northward via Wilderspool, Wigan, Walton-le-Dale, and heading ultimately for Carlisle; another from the Wall area, via Chesterton and Middlewich and hence also to the Mersey. Yet another route ran north-eastward through Middlewich to Manchester, and then on to Ribchester, Burrow-in-Lonsdale and beyond.

Although developments there were clearly influential, how Chester fitted into all this remains unclear. It has been noted that the newly built legionary fortress there is too far out on a western limb to be of direct geographical relevance in the anticipated overland campaigning. It seems that Chester's prime function was to be a maritime one, and the main road from Wroxeter to Chester may also have become important in the logistical support of the fleet. Nonetheless, we should also assume that the regulation, ordering, administrative and logistical support must have been based there and to have emanated from the offices in the legion's headquarters-building (*principia*). Wroxeter began to seem rather distant, to the rear. The newly-built regimental fort at Middlewich may well have fallen under the new Chester Command.

Once again, Middlewich played its part in a great northward advance by the Roman Army. Those soldiers based there will have been actively associated with facilitating the advance, and keeping watch over the area, including the temporary accommodation, in tented camps for a great army on the move. Such marching-camps at Middlewich remain uncertain but seem reasonable and may be hinted at in the area east of King Street and in the Church Fields area to the south of the river-crossings. There was, too, the salt – as ever, a valuable commodity and now controlled to some extent, but not exclusively, by the Army. However, the legionary element, which had been so conspicuous in the early 70s campaign against the *Brigantes*, appears to have been much reduced in the establishment at Middlewich.

The infrastructure of communications and supply-roads in the region was developed further in the aftermath of the construction of Chester and its sister-fortress at York, across the Pennines. Thus, for example, new roads were driven eastward from Chester to Manchester, via a new regimental fort at Northwich. Curiously, this road and the military dispositions along it seem to bear no logical relation to the Middlewich – Warrington Road, suggesting that Middlewich was temporarily relegated to a secondary status – one more explicitly associated with logistics perhaps – in the new campaign. But the great road north via Wilderspool continued as an important logistical artery; a fact which is indicated by new direct roads built from Chester to both Middlewich and Wilderspool.

The Emperor Vespasian died in June 79 when the Army was already on the edge of the Scottish Highlands, along the River Tay. Under his son, Titus, Agricola was encouraged to consolidate his hold on the Southern Uplands and Central Lowlands. But, on that new emperor's premature death in 81, his younger brother, Domitian, who was interested in and very popular with the Army, demanded a further advance. Thus, by 84, the Romans were up near Inverness and had engaged the tribes in a great battle, somewhere perhaps in the northern Grampians.

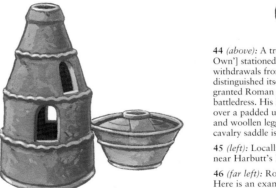

44 *(above):* A trooper from the ALA CLASSIANA ['Classius's Own'] stationed at Middlewich in c.AD 100, as a result of troop-withdrawals from Scotland. This cavalry regiment appears to have distinguished itself in the northern fighting, for which it was granted Roman citizenship status. The trooper is shown in battledress. His helmet is of iron and bronze. He wears a mailshirt over a padded undergarment, a red military tunic, short trousers and woollen leggings. His boots are spurred. A four-horned cavalry saddle is visible but, it will be noted, no stirrups are used.

45 *(left):* Locally made chimney-pot and wine-cooler, found near Harbutt's Field 1998–1999.

46 *(far left):* Roman-type chimney-pots are still used in Italy. Here is an example from Lunigiana.

The great battle was fought and won by the auxiliary regiments but, as events were to prove, it was not a decisive victory and Agricola was recalled to Rome soon afterwards, his much-extended term of governorship concluded. And then, a major war broke out on the Danube front, where Germanic tribes broke through and inflicted serious defeats on the Romans in 85. Domitian sought further reinforcements with some desperation, and a number of important units, among them the Second *Adiutrix* Legion, were hurriedly withdrawn from Britain.

The northward British advance ground to a halt, with inadequate direction and resources to achieve a military conclusion. Then in 86–7, further fighting across the Rhine and, subsequently, on the Danube led to another defeat for Roman Arms. The impact on Britain was considerable: construction of the new legionary fortress at Inchtuthill (VICTORIA), on the Tay, was abandoned unfinished, and the depleted Roman Army of Britain gradually withdrew southward. By 90, the Twentieth Legion had withdrawn to Chester, its old base at Wroxeter having been given up to what would soon become the new Roman administrative centre of the *Cornovii*. Other units also moved southward, and Middlewich was likewise affected by them. It became the base for another auxiliary regiment, perhaps the ALA CLASSIANA CIVIUM ROMANORUM ('Classianus's Own, Roman Citizens') – one of the crack cavalry wings.

47 *(above left):* Examples of late first – early second century pottery found at Middlewich (including locally made grey-wares, orange-wares made both locally and at Holt, a grinding-bowl (*mortarium*) imported from Hertfordshire).

48 *(above):* Pottery from a possible Roman grave, found at Kinderton in 1997.

49 *(below):* Late first – early second century glass unguent bottles and containers found at Middlewich.

50 *(left):* The southwest corner of the defences of the Roman auxiliary regimental fort at Harbutt's Field, overlooking the River Croco at Middlewich, in c.AD 100. In the foreground is a trooper from the ALA CLASSIANA cavalry regiment. Behind him, parties of Roman soldiers are at work in repair-and-maintenance of the fort. The defensive ditches were re-cut at this time.

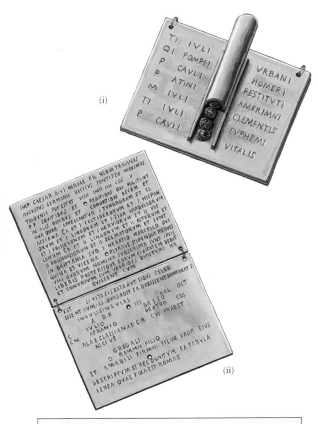

(i)

(ii)

THE MIDDLEWICH DIPLOMA

One of the most interesting finds is a fragment of a Roman military discharge diploma relating to the period in which units of the Roman Army were stationed at Middlewich. This confirms a grant of Roman citizenship to a retired trooper from the ALA CLASSIANA in AD 105. Diplomas [from a Greek word meaning 'folded over'], confirming a grant of citizenship and its important rights, were given to auxiliary soldiers on retirement, normally after 25 years service. Bronze was used for durability since the document was a very important one. To prevent damage the diploma was then folded over and sealed by witnesses. Details on the front summarized its contents.

TRANSLATION

Although only a fragment of the diploma survives it has been possible to reconstruct most of the missing portions of a standardised text from other, more complete, examples. Here is the translation [surviving words printed in **bold**].

'The Emperor Caesar Nerva Traianus Augustus, conqueror of Germany, conqueror of Dacia, chief priest, in his ninth year of tribunician power, four times acclaimed victorious, five times consul, father of his country, has granted to the cavalrymen and infantrymen who are serving in [*number unknown*] alae and [*number unknown*] cohorts called; ala Gallorum et Thracum Classiana, Roman Citizens and [*unit names unknown*], and who are stationed in Britain under [*governor's name unknown*], who have served 25 or more years, and whose names are written below:

Citizenship for themselves, their children and descendants, and the right of legal marriage with the wives they had when the citizenship was granted to them, **or**, if any were unmarried, **with those who they later marry, so long as it is only one each. Given this day [three or four days before....]** in the consulships of Caius Julius Bassus and Gnaeus Afranius Dexter (*AD 105, 4 May–13 July*)

From .....ala Classiana, Roman Citizens, commander **......nicius**

To the cavalryman called .....us, son of Rammus (?) from (?) and A**mabilis, daughter of Firmus**, his wife. **Copied and checked** from the bronze tablet **set up in Rome.**

(Witnesses) Tiberius Ju**lius** Urbanus, Quintus Po**mpeius** Homerus, Publius C**aulius** Restitutus, Publius Atinius Amerimnus, **Marcus Julius** Clemens, **Tiberius Julius** Euphemus, Publius Caulius Vitalis'

51 *(above left)*: Reconstructions of the Middlewich diploma based on the remarkable discovery of the most complete example known whilst dredging for sand in the bed of the River Sava, near Slavonski Brod in Croatia, in 1997. This example even included the wax impressions of the seals of the witnesses, and sliding protective cover.

(i) The diploma folded, showing the names of the witnesses in Rome and the sliding seals cover. The folded diploma measured approximately 160mm x 130mm.

(ii) The two bronze leaves of the diploma, opened out to reveal the full text of the formal grant of Roman citizenship to the recipient.

THE ALA CLASSIANA

Otherwise known as the...

ALA GALLORUM ET THRACUM CLASSIANA INVICTA BIS TORQUATA CIVIUM ROMANORUM

The full title of the cavalry regiment can be translated as.. '*Classius's Own cavalry regiment of Gauls and Thracians, twice mentioned-in-despatches, honorary Roman citizens*'.

This distinguished unit was raised originally in Gaul [France], by one Classius, during the early first century AD, and was later strengthened with a Thracian contingent [from NE Greece and Bulgaria]. It was, of course, recruiting locally and more widely by the time of its posting to Britain. It is first recorded in Britain, on the Middlewich diploma, in 105 but had clearly already been here for some time, even possibly since the Claudian invasion of 43, or perhaps since the northern campaigning in the 70's. For meritorious war-service in northern Britain in the late first century it was mentioned in despatches and awarded a block-grant of Roman citizenship. At some stage between the 90s and the early second century the unit may have been stationed at Middlewich, possibly as a result of Domitian's withdrawals from Scotland but, until more conclusive evidence comes to light, this will remain uncertain. The regiment was still in Britain in 122 although it was posted away soon afterwards, perhaps along with other British units, for Hadrian's Jewish War in 132. It later served in Lower Germany and did not return to Britain.

52 *(above):* Front and rear views of a fragment of one side of the bronze military discharge diploma found off King Street, Middlewich, in 1939. This confirms the Emperor Trajan's grant of Roman citizenship to a retired trooper from the ALA CLASSIANA cavalry regiment in AD 105.

53 *(above right):* Drawing clarifying the surviving lettering on the Middlewich diploma fragment. By comparison with other, more complete, examples, it is possible to work out what the missing text would have said [except, unfortunately, the name of the man who owned it].

54 *(right):* The retired veteran from the ALA CLASSIANA proudly shows his discharge diploma to his family and informs them that they are all now Roman citizens. This veteran may have retired to Middlewich to engage in the salt-business.

The saltworks establishment adjacent to the fort, still at this time a primarily military concern, fell again under the Chester Command, this time the Twentieth Legion.

Domitian was assassinated in 96, much to the Army's disgust, and, after a brief reign by Nerva, Trajan became emperor in 98. There is a hint of further trouble in Britain at this time, perhaps the northern *Brigantes* were still restless, and there was some serious, if shortlived action. But Trajan had ambitions elsewhere – renewed war across the Danube (101–106), then Armenia and major war into Mesopotamia, which took the Romans beyond Baghdad (106–117).

We hear little of Britain in this period although the military presence at Middlewich continued, and the saltworks developed further under military control. Retired soldiers from the auxiliary regiments, in possession of their savings and gratuities, were also settling in the area and perhaps marrying local *Cornovian* women. Such men, among them at least one veteran from the ALA CLASSIANA, may have been going into the salt-business as private operators and entrepreneurs.

Trajan died in 117 and was succeeded by Hadrian. The Empire had been exhausted by Trajan's great and expensive campaigns, and Hadrian considered further conquest undesirable. He had other ideas, among them the establishment of physical limits to the Roman World. In the years that followed, things would change at Middlewich.

55 *(above):* Roman legionary citizen-soldier in full parade order. At various times during the late first and early second centuries such soldiers had passed through Middlewich.

56 *(above right):* Soon after the accession of the Emperor Hadrian in AD 117, the regiment which had been stationed at Middlewich appears to have been withdrawn. Prior to their departure, the soldiers dismantled the fort at Harbutt's Field.

57 *(right):* Middlewich in c.AD 100. From the late 80s the Romans withdrew gradually from Scotland and many units had to be relocated southward as a result. This process led to a resurgence of military activity at Middlewich. In this scene, a permanent fort for an auxiliary regiment has been built within the confluence of the Rivers Dane and Croco, where Harbutt's Field is now situated. Some of the old British Cornovian trackways have been upgraded by the Roman Army into all-weather roads. The King Street area has been demarcated for the rapidly developing military saltworks. On the whole, peaceful relations continue with the local tribal community who also continue to exploit the salt brine-springs.

III
ROMAN MIDDLEWICH AD 122–C.260

58 *(above)*: The Emperor Hadrian (117–138) visited Britain in 122. Under him construction started on Hadrian's Wall. He also initiated great changes throughout the province, and these influenced events at Middlewich for many years. By c.150 the place was flourishing.

59 *(below)*: Northwestern Britain during the late second – early third centuries. The infrastructure has developed further and civilian settlements have supplanted auxiliary forts in many places. Among them, the saltworking establishments flourished in central Cheshire.

Circa AD 150–250

- ■ Legionary Fortress
- ■ Fort
- □ Possible Fortlet
- ● Cantonal Capital
- ● Other Setlement
- ● Other Setlement (Salt)
- —— Roman Road (certain)
- - - Roman Road (possible)

0 10 20 30miles

CARLISLE

BURROW-IN-LONSDALE
Alone?

MORECAMBE BAY
Moricambus Aest.

LANCASTER
Galacum?

RIBCHESTER
Bremetennacum

WALTON-LE-DALE

WIGAN
Coccium

MANCHESTER
Mamuclum

Seteia

Meols

Wilderspool

ANGLESEY
Mona

PRESTATYN

ST. ASAPH
Varae?

NORTHWICH
Condate?

BUXTON

CAERHUN
Canovium

CHESTER
Deva

MIDDLEWICH
Salinae?

CAERNARFON
Segontium

BRYN-Y-GEFEILIAU

HOLT
Bovium

Nantwich Shavington

Deva

HOLDITCH

TOMEN-Y-MUR

WHITCHURCH
Mediolanum

CAER GAI

BRITHDIR

WROXETER
Viroconium

PENKRIDGE
Pennocrucium

WALL
Letocetvm

In this chapter the second and third century heyday of Middlewich is described. It was initially a result of the Emperor Hadrian's reforms but it continued to be stimulated by logistical and supply requirements associated with troop-movements, frontier-works and campaigns in northern Britain throughout the second century. Perhaps the civil war and ultimate clash in 197 between Clodius Albinus, Governor of Britain, and Septimius Severus was a serious setback for Britain but it was not to last. With Severus's campaigns in Britain in the early third century confidence was restored and Middlewich continued to flourish. The devolution of Britain into two smaller provinces followed. This may also have stimulated further development at Middlewich, not far from a new administrative border on the Mersey. After the assassination of Alexander Severus in 235 the Empire experienced the onset of a new, grimmer world of Germanic tribal incursions, rough soldier-emperors and spectacular defeats. Middlewich survived, but by the 260s a long slow decline had set in.

In his celebrated visit to Britain in 122 the Emperor Hadrian set about the reorganisation of the province. Most famous was the construction of Hadrian's Wall which demonstrated the new emperor's determination to set definable and controllable limits to the Empire. Behind the Wall, Hadrian set about the stimulation of the development of Roman civilization. The erection of his great new inscription over the newly built Forum at Wroxeter may even imply the Emperor's personal attention – and certainly his interest – in supporting and guiding the growth and architectural adornment of the new cantonal capital of the *Cornovii* (VIROCONIUM CORNOVIORUM). Middlewich was on the most direct road (via Whitchurch) to Wroxeter and if Hadrian did not visit Chester he might well have passed through the settlement: an interesting possibility. In any event, Middlewich products [especially salt] would have been on sale in the markets of the great new city and centre of local government only some 40 miles – and two days' journey – away.

Apart from his military concerns and interests, Hadrian's reforms were directed at the peaceful development and 'Romanisation' of the province, and Middlewich would have benefited from this. At some stage after his visit to Britain, however, the regiment which had been stationed at Middlewich was withdrawn, perhaps in preparation for the Jewish War of 132, in which other units from Britain were involved. Nonetheless, military interest in the place must have continued, in particular on account of the salt but also because of its strategically important location. In this period *Cornovians* were also joining the Army: a development which is attested by the formation of COHORS I CORNOVIORUM ('The First Cornovians') who appear to have been stationed for a time at Newcastle-upon-Tyne. Thus the old cultural distinctions between Roman, and Briton continued to be broken down.

Under the Emperor Antoninus Pius (136–161) much of Scotland was reoccupied, and a new frontier – the

60 *(left)*: Hoard of silver denarii buried intentionally near Harbutt's Field some years after 125, and rediscovered in 1998. Such coins often represent Army pay or at least military transactions, but the circumstances of the burial remain unknown.

Antonine Wall – built. This seems to have been associated with further trouble among the northern *Brigantes*. Under Marcus Aurelius (161–180) the northern troubles continued, leading to major tribal incursions into the province in 180; and under Commodus (180–192) the problems, whatever they were, persisted. We know little of Middlewich in this period except that saltworking there was in full swing and the settlement was expanding steadily. Much of this evident prosperity and development must have been related to the major troop and logistical movements, arising from the northern campaigning, and sustained over several decades. Army administrative involvement in at least some of this activity is likely.

The assassination of the Emperor Commodus in 192 plunged the entire Roman World into civil war: this time a fearsome war which lasted for several years, and in which the great army-commanders vied for the purple. What might be termed the final episode in this great upheaval was perhaps the most traumatic for Britain. This started when Clodius Albinus, Governor of Britain, stripped the province of troops (including the legions) in his bid to become emperor. Under Albinus, the soldiers embarked on a great campaign in Gaul, which ended, at Lyons in 197, in his crushing defeat, and the near destruction of his army, by Septimius Severus. The decimation of the Army of Britain and, of particular significance to the *Cornovians*, the Twentieth Legion, whose depot had long been at Chester, must have been shattering. It must also have had a great impact on the surrounding area: on important activities like the procurement of salt and,

61 Stages in the Roman saltmaking process.

1. Brine from spring is collected in holding-tank or well.
2. Brine is removed from holding-tank in wooden bucket.
3. Brine simmering in salt-pan.
4. Salt residue is removed from pan after brine has been boiled off.
5. Collecting salt prior to removal from site.
6. Transportation of salt in baskets and sacks.

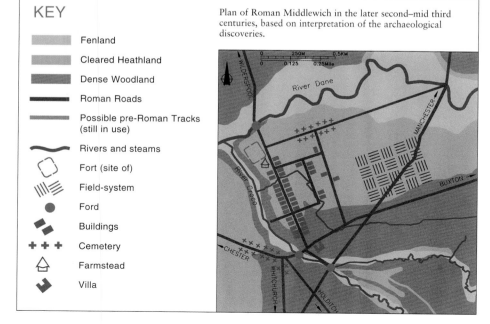

KEY

	Fenland
	Cleared Heathland
	Dense Woodland
	Roman Roads
	Possible pre-Roman Tracks (still in use)
	Rivers and steams
	Fort (site of)
	Field-system
	Ford
	Buildings
	Cemetery
	Farmstead
	Villa

Plan of Roman Middlewich in the later second–mid third centuries, based on interpretation of the archaeological discoveries.

62 *(left):* Bar from a salt-working site off King Street, 1960.

63 *(right):* The Army had moved away from Middlewich by c.130, probably as a result of Hadrian's policies, and a large settlement developed alongside King Street as a result. This settlement was essentially a civilian one in which the old distinctions between 'Roman' and 'Cornovian' gradually disappeared through the extension of citizenship and inter-marriage. Although saltworking was the major activity there is also evidence of both leatherworking and ironsmithing. However, the latter may have been no more than one would expect in any such settlement of this period, when a considerable degree of self-sufficiency was essential. In this scene, the ribbon development along King Street is viewed from west of the River Croco in the late second – early third centuries. Note the brine holding-tanks, wells, lifting-devices and brine-boiling activity.

64

65

64 Clay-lined brine holding-tank discovered at Kinderton Hall Farm in 1999.

65 Briquetage vessel incorporated into the clay lining of a brine holding-tank, Kinderton Hall Farm in 1999. [*Briquetage = rough baked clay linings, bars, bricks, containers, etc. associated with salt-production.]

66 *(right):* A South Spanish olive-oil container re-used at Middlewich for collecting waste material from the saltworks, indicated by the graffito 'AMVRCA'.

67 *(above):* The 'AMVRCA' graffito on a South Spanish amphora as it would have appeared when freshly painted. 'AMVRCA' means 'for collecting waste from brine'.

68 *(right):* In the third century the area to the north of Kinderton Hall Farm continued to be used as a cemetery. Fragmentary cremation-urn discovered in roadside ditch there, in 1999.

69 *(above):* A selection of objects discovered by metal-detectorists off King Street, 1998–2000: second century bronze brooches.

70 *(right):* A second century gold finger-ring found off King Street, 1964–1969.

72 *(above):* Examples of vessels reaching Middlewich from elsewhere in Britain during the third century. Including cooking-jars from Yorkshire, Lincolnshire and Derbyshire; grinding-bowls (mortaria) from the Midlands; and decorated 'hunt' cups from the Nene Valley, near Peterborough.

71 *(above):* By the middle of the second century, a considerable saltworks establishment had developed along King Street. In this scene, based closely on discoveries made in the area, salt is under production. In the foreground, brine is being lifted from a timber-revetted holding-tank; on the right a brine-kiln is in operation, with briquetage salt-pans being heated. Old storage-jars (amphorae), being used for 'brine waste', are scattered throughout the yard. Although the old fort at Harbutt's Field is no longer in operation, military interest in securing a regular supply of salt is indicated by the officer making records and keeping tallies.

73 *(left):* Examples of the large containers (amphorae) reaching Middlewich in the period c.200–c.250 with a wide range of specialities. These included various fruits, capers and alum from the central Mediterranean islands; olive-oil from southern Spain; sweet wine from southern France.

74 The Emperor Septimius Severus (193–211) was another strong and decisive ruler. He also initiated great changes in Britain. He came to Britain [and may also have visited the Chester area] in 208–211, with his Syrian wife and sons, intent upon the total conquest of Scotland. In the aftermath of his visit, renewed activity at Chester shows that he had stimulated further development in the area, and no doubt also at Middlewich. This heightened activity continued for the next thirty years or so.

75 Under reforms initiated by Septimius Severus, Britannia was subdivided into two different, smaller provinces. Middlewich fell within BRITANNIA SUPERIOR. The western border between the two probably fell along the Mersey, and Middlewich – still on the main road north – may well have benefited from the administrative changes.

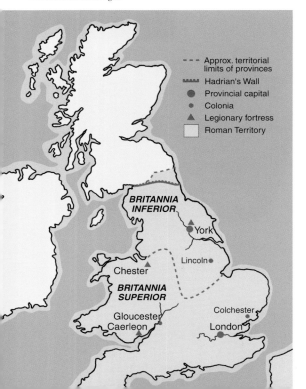

- - - Approx. territorial limits of provinces
〰 Hadrian's Wall
● Provincial capital
• Colonia
▲ Legionary fortress
▢ Roman Territory

not least, on those families whose fathers, sons and relatives served with the eagle.

Serious trouble in the North, perhaps associated with the Albinus episode, would eventually lead Septimius Severus to Britain, intent upon its total subjugation. Thus, from 208–211, the emperor campaigned in Scotland, together with his Syrian wife and sons; and with all the logistical and supply implications for places like Middlewich. But Septimius died in York soon afterwards, with the fulfilment of his objectives incomplete, and the empress and his sons returned to Italy.

In the years that followed, Britain was divided into two smaller provinces, as much as anything to ensure that no new provincial governor would be as strong as Albinus had been. Middlewich was then not far distant from a new provincial administrative border on the Mersey. Of greater and more lasting significance, under the *constitutio antoniniana* all free-born peoples of the Roman World were elevated to the Roman citizenship. The previous distinctions between Roman and Briton were thus broken down further still. From this moment the people of Middlewich were Romans.

The energetic rebuilding and development of the provinces of Britannia, initiated by Septimius and his sons, continued for some years to follow, and the growth of the Middlewich saltworks continued. But the death of Severus Alexander [the last of the Severan dynasty] in 235, assassinated by his own troops on the Rhine frontier led, in the west, to what has been called Rome's 'Age of Crisis'. More significant for us, the dirty deed had been carried out, in the face of a serious threat from the *Alamanni* [a German tribal confederation], at a place called *Vicus Britannicus* [British township] near Mainz.

The 'Age of Crisis' followed, in which soldier-emperor after soldier-emperor had to contend with twin, simultaneous menaces on the German and Eastern fronts. The Empire reached its lowest ebb. In the west, the mounting pressures of Germanic immigration, among them a massive incursion by *Alamanni* in 258, nearly tore the Empire apart. Out of this near chaos emerged Cassianius Postumus, Rhine army-commander, who established an independent 'Gallic Empire' of which Britain was a part. This would last, with mixed success, for sixteen years. But constant change, increasing insecurity, breakdown of infrastructure, more administrative change, devolution and inflationary pressures all had negative impacts. Middlewich would survive the 'Age of Crisis' but its continued development had been arrested. A long slow decline had set in.

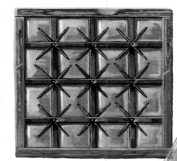

76 Reconstruction of a Roman window based on fragments of glass discovered near King Street in recent years. Other related finds have suggested there was a bath-house somewhere in that area during the second and third centuries.

77 *(right)*: Middlewich in the early third century. The Roman Army no longer operates from a fort at Harbutt's Field although it still retains an interest in the area. Instead, Middlewich is now dominated by a saltworks establishment which has grown as a ribbon development astride the main road (King Street). This road is still an important artery along which goods of all kinds, many of them destined for military use, continue to be moved. The old Cornovian community still flourishes in the neighbourhood but it has become increasingly 'Romanised' in its way of life. Note also the cemetery along the road heading eastward beside the River Dane.

IV
LATE ROMAN MIDDLEWICH

78 *(above):* The Emperor Diocletian (284–305) [from a coin-portrait]. He completely reorganised the Roman World after the 'Age of Crisis' and, in so doing, gave it a new lease of life. But his fundamental reforms further stimulated the fall into totalitarian dictatorship. Diocletian retired to Spalatum [Split] in 305 and died there in 316.

79 *(below):* Northwestern Britain in the fourth Century.

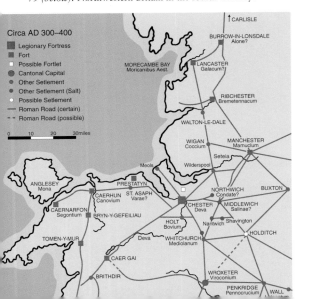

This chapter reviews events from just after Rome's 'Age of Crisis' in the middle of the third century, to the late fourth century. In this period Rome slowly recovered but re-emerged from it much changed. The years after Diocletian's accession in 284 saw the complete reorganisation of the Empire. For a few years in the later third century Britain formed a part of the breakaway empire of Carausius and Allectus, but in 296 central government control was restored by Constantius Chlorus. Decline at Middlewich continued through the fourth century and the saltworks contracted to a small-scale operation. The Christian community may have been involved at this time, even perhaps a Christian bishop.

The western provinces of the Roman Empire slowly recovered from the Age of Crisis in the later years of the third century. This was achieved largely by a series of fighting soldier – emperors who, for a time it seemed, had stemmed the tide of Germanic immigration from across the Rhine and Danube. But, as is the way of these things, out of this very success and survival the Rome which re-emerged was a very different place, and a very different world: one which seems to be more an ancestor of the Middle Ages than the descendant of Julius Caesar and Hadrian. In fact, of course, it was both these things, more a kind of half-way house, with some of the qualities of both past and future. These years of the later third century [268–284 to be precise] are often described as the 'Age of Recovery', and it was a remarkable recovery indeed, despite what was lost – or changed – in its progress. But at the end of it, even mighty Rome herself was surrounded, and protected, by a great defensive fortification – the Walls of Aurelian – so uncertain and dangerous had the times become.

And then in 284, emerged Diocletian, born of Dalmatian peasant stock, who, having risen to high command in the Army, was hailed emperor by his soldiers at Nicomedia [Izmit in Turkey]. During his reign the whole Empire was reconstructed and reorganised. It was, nonetheless, a grimmer world: one of ever-shrinking economy, devolutionary pressures, Germanic immigration, and [of perhaps even greater significance for the future] a failure to come to terms with these immigrants, either culturally or racially. In the process, the Roman Army itself, for so long a remarkable achievement, was changed fundamentally as well; not least as a result of the very success of recruitment from among the Germanic peoples of the frontier-zones, who had clamoured to join it for so long.

For a time, Britain and part of northern Gaul broke away from legitimate Roman government under Mausaeus Carausius, a general with a background of distinguished and successful service in Gaul, who had risen to command of the Channel Fleet. Under him, the provinces of Britannia seem to have been well managed and well protected from the pirates [Franks, Saxons and others] who increasingly infested the North Sea and Channel coasts, on the one hand, and from raiders across the Irish Sea [Scots] on the other. Against both, the protection of the fleet became ever more essential.

There is no specific evidence relating to these years at Middlewich but coins of Carausius have turned up in sufficient quantity at Chester to indicate that soldiers were still being regularly paid there; and the implication must be that places like Chester, erstwhile legionary fortress [whatever that means at this date is unclear] were used as bases in the control of piracy. Middlewich, in the hinterland, cannot have been entirely unaffected.

80 *(left)*: Iron shears found amongst other fourth century material off King Street, 1964–1969.

Carausius was assassinated by Allectus, his deputy and financial official, in 296. Constantius Chlorus, Caesar of the West, then invaded southern Britain with a great fleet and army, and restored the provinces to central Roman control: what is described on one remarkable golden medallion, struck to commemorate the victory, as 'The Restoration of the Eternal Light'. Political confidence and conviction indeed! But it was not the reality, and within a few years Britain was being ravaged by a new menace – the Picts – out of Caledonia [the Highlands of Scotland]. In 306 Constantius returned to Britain with his son Constantine, and campaigned successfully in the North. How this campaigning, with its many logistical implications, affected Middlewich is unknown, and it may be that much of the activity associated with it went via York. There it was that Constantius died and Constantine was proclaimed Emperor by the Army of Britain.

In this period, undoubtedly in response to Diocletian's political and military re-organisation, Britain was further subdivided into four provinces. Cheshire fell within BRITANNIA PRIMA, whose northern and eastern boundaries were on the Mersey and in the Pennines respectively. Once again, the impact of these changes on Middlewich is unclear but we may surmise that changes there were. Although they may have seemed appropriate, even inevitable, at the time, the changes will have served also to increase bureaucratic interference, increase taxation, increase the role of the State in people's lives, and restrict what we might call 'freedom'. Furthermore, the breakdown into smaller

81 *(above)*: In the fourth century lead had replaced briquetage as the material preferred for use in salt-pans at Middlewich. On this one is moulded the name LVTAMI ['property of Lutamus']. Lutamus was probably an entrepreneur operating at the Middlewich saltworks.

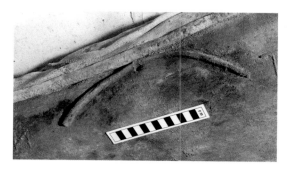

82 *(above)*: Fourth century salt-pans were clearly designed to be lifted, or suspended, with iron hooks, as this detail of one end of a salt-pan demonstrates.

83 *(below)*: In the earlier fourth century the large pottery-producing centres were still in operation and their products continued to reach Middlewich. Examples of black-burnished jars and bowls from Dorset, and a grinding-bowl [*mortarium*] from the Midlands, found at Middlewich.

KEY

	Fenland
	Cleared Heathland
	Open Woodland
	Dense Woodland
	Roman Roads
	Possible pre-Roman Tracks (still in use)
	Rivers and streams
	Fort (site of)
	Ford
	Buildings
+++	Cemetery
△	Farmstead

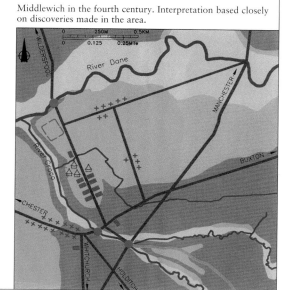

Middlewich in the fourth century. Interpretation based closely on discoveries made in the area.

84 Late Roman lead salt-pans were often cast with the names of the entrepreneurs who operated the saltworks, sometimes on leases from the State. This example, discovered near Shavington, folded for re-use or sale elsewhere for its scrap-value, has the name FL VIVENTIVS [Flavius Viventius] moulded along one side. Intriguingly, this is a 'Christian' name and demonstrates that Christians were involved in at least some of the saltworks in the fourth century.

85 By the fourth century Britain had been subdivided into four small provinces, and Middlewich was in the province of BRITANNIA PRIMA, with its capital at Cirencester, in Gloucestershire.

86 This late Roman lead salt-pan, found near Shavington, had been cut up into sections for re-use – or sale – at a later date. Along one side, the words VIVENT...COPI had been cast. Here again, is confirmation of one VIVENTIUS, a Christian, involved in saltworking in the fourth century. But, even more important,...COPI is probably a fragment of the word EPISCOPI which implies that Viventius was either a bishop or operating on behalf of one.

units, itself initially a pragmatic response to emerging pressures, must have served also to reduce people's horizons, culturally, politically and economically.

Meanwhile, life continued at Middlewich, but although the settlement had survived the 'Age of Crisis' a long slow decline in its commercial activities had set in. Saltworking continued along King Street but on a much reduced scale further to the south, nearer the junction of King Street with the Buxton road [now Kinderton Street], perhaps because that area was closer to a convenient crossing-point on the River Croco. Coins were still circulating in the settlement, with the related commercial and tax implications, down to at least the 350s.

In this period it seems that briquetage, the baked clay originally used for linings and containers in the saltworks, was being replaced by lead as the preferred material in salt-pans; a distinctive feature of the late Roman Cheshire saltings. But in some ways it is a surprising development, and archaeology may one day change this picture, for lead had been mined by the Romans in North Wales, and extensively used for other purposes in the region, since the first century. Be that as it may, such lead salt-pans have been found at Middlewich, Northwich, Nantwich and Shavington, where they give a fortunate insight into the saltworking, for the names of some of the operators are cast, and preserved, on them. Among these, one LUTAMUS, no doubt an entrepreneur or leaseholder from the State, was operating at Middlewich. There is, too, some indication that among these individuals, or proprietors, were those who had a Celtic ancestry: such a man was CUNITUS [a Romanised Celtic name] at Nantwich. VELUVIUS at Northwich may have been another. There is nothing surprising about this, for the Roman Empire had been a catalyst for such mixing for centuries. It is thus entirely reasonable to assume that the racial and cultural implications of this applied also at Middlewich, where the old cultural distinctions between Roman and Briton had all but disappeared long before, except perhaps in the remoter farmsteads where a more traditional culture continued.

87 *(right):* Discoveries at Shavington, near Nantwich, have demonstrated that some of the saltworks in central Cheshire were under the control of a Christian community in the fourth century. Given the continuing political and administrative importance of Chester at that time, amongst other things as the probable centre of the Christian Church in the area, prelates of the Church may well have taken an interest in the saltworks. In this scene, a bishop from Chester crosses the River Croco at Middlewich, where a Christian community may also have been operating.

88 *(above):* A Christian prelate discusses provision of salt to the community at Chester.

89 *(below):* Major centres of Christianity in late Roman Britain.

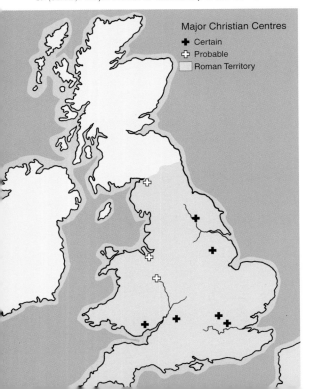

Major Christian Centres
✚ Certain
⛨ Probable
▢ Roman Territory

The Emperor Constantine's Edict of Milan declared Christianity a favoured religion in 313 and, within a few decades, Britain was officially – but by no means exclusively – Christian. There had, of course, long been Christians in the region, a fact hinted at by some enigmatic evidence from Manchester, as early as the late second century, and it is reasonable to assume that there had also been small, but growing, Christian communities elsewhere in the area: the result of its introduction by soldiers and traders. Intriguingly, however, there is explicit evidence of the Christian community, active in saltworking in central Cheshire – from Shavington, near Nantwich. Its possible implications for Middlewich are of such interest that some mention of them is appropriate.

From the Shavington-Nantwich area have come fragments of no less than three late-Roman lead salt-pans associated with the Christian Church. Thus, the name of the Romanised Celt, CUNITUS, appears on one pan with the letters CLER, probably an abbreviation for CLERICUS, meaning Christian 'cleric' or 'priest'. The other two pans provide us with something more: for it seems that one FL [Flavius?] VIVENTIUS, the bearer of a well known 'Christian' name, which appears on both, was either a bishop, or associated with and working for one, in the local saltworks: one of the pans cast with his name is followed by…COPI, surely a fragment of the word EPISCOPI, meaning 'bishop' or 'on behalf of the bishop'.

Given the continuing importance of Chester, its proximity and the likely presence of a large Christian community there in this period, it seems entirely appropriate for the Church to have maintained an interest in the saltworks from at least the later fourth century. In many ways, of course, the Church was developing into a kind of reflection of the Roman State, even a means of administrative continuity, and it is intriguing to think that VIVENTIUS might have been an early bishop at Chester and that the Middlewich saltings might have been of interest to him.

Thus we can infer that some of the Middlewich saltworks continued to operate down to at least the later fourth century. But we should remember that the place had never been exclusively preoccupied with salt-production, for there is also evidence of tanning and leatherworking, weaving, cobbling, copperworking and ironworking from different parts of the settlement, at different dates. This activity may seem widespread but we must be careful to avoid the word 'industry' in describing it. It is present in every small settlement where, even in living memory, small communities had to be more or less self-sufficient. The archaeological evidence may not mean more than this.

The brine-kilns were in operation down to at least the later fourth century. However, what may be described as quality imports had ceased to reach Middlewich: clearly the place had reverted to one of only regional, or even local, importance. The long, slow contraction in the settlement was far advanced, and living standards had been falling steadily. People were being buried in derelict areas of the settlement. Others had been drifting away to what had become more certain means of livelihood. By the beginning of the fifth century Middlewich was a pale reflection of what it had once been. Instead, we can imagine a return to dispersed agricultural activity and a going back to cultural roots: people are great survivors.

90 *(right):* Middlewich in the fourth century. Although the saltworks establishment still operates it is much reduced in size and population. The main road to the North [King Street] is still important, and so also is the road to Chester.

V
ENDS AND
BEGINNINGS

91 *(above):* The Emperor Honorius (395–423) [from a coin-portrait]. During his reign the Goths sacked Rome and when, in 410, the British authorities sought assistance from him, in a famous *Rescript*, he ordered them to fend for themselves. The result was the end of direct rule from the Continent, an event which is often described as the end of Roman Britain.

92 *(below):* Northwestern Britain in the fifth and sixth centuries. By this date British Kingdoms, based originally on late Roman political arrangements and evolutionary processes, had begun to emerge. Although no longer maintained, the main Roman roads continued to facilitate travel through the region.

This is the period in which Roman historical fact merges with Celtic British legend. With the sack of Rome by the Goths in 410, appeals by the British authorities fell increasingly on deaf ears. But out of late Roman political arrangements emerged Celtic British Kingdoms, in one of which – Powys – Cheshire lay. This remained the case until sometime before the middle of the seventh century when the area fell within English territory. It was not an end: a hundred years later, the beginnings of modern Middlewich would emerge.

The closing years of the fourth century witnessed further troubles in Britain and, on various occasions, major military campaigns in the North. Perhaps the most celebrated, and in some ways most significant for us, are those associated with Count Theodosius and his protégé, Magnus Maximus, between 369 and 383 – for this is the point at which Roman historical fact merges with and becomes Celtic British legend. Magnus Maximus, Roman general and Commander-in-Chief of the armies in Britain, has archaeologically proven connections with North Wales [his coins were used to pay troops there]. He will become MACSEN WLEDIG [Great Macsen] in the legend, husband of Elen, daughter of a British Prince or King, and ancestor of Arthur. Thus, in both fact and legend, Maximus took troops from Britain to the Continent where, after ruling as Emperor at Trier on the Moselle, he was defeated and killed and his British soldiers never returned. Curiously, this story is supported by some negative evidence from Chester where, despite much interest in this episode over many years, not one of Maximus's silver coins has been found: if these coins were in circulation to pay troops, no troops were being paid with them at Chester. Had what was left of the garrison there already departed?

Finally, direct government of the provinces of Britain from the Continent ceased in the early fifth century. It had been rendered impractical by the growing pressures of Germanic immigration. This had, of course, been going on for centuries – especially through recruitment to the Army – but by the fifth century the scale of it was enormous and out of control. Furthermore, the expedient increasingly adopted by impoverished government of giving land to the newcomers, in return for military service and peace, was also contributing to irreversible changes. Rome, which for so long had accommodated and swallowed all these things was now being swallowed herself.

In Britain, the authorities hung on somehow in the face of increasing threats and devolutionary pressures on all sides; early in the fifth century they sought the assistance of the Emperor Honorius in the time-honoured manner. But, in 410, Rome herself was sacked by bands of marauding Goths and the emperor, in desperation, replied that he could not help, in the famous *Rescript*. In the years that followed there may have been some restored contact but this is the period in which 'Roman Britain' is considered to have come to an end: nothing sudden or specific, more a gradual 'fizzling-out' or evolution into something else.

Thus, in Britain, the fifth century saw the emergence of Celtic British Kingdoms, themselves descended perhaps from late Roman devolutionary political arrangements. In this period, Cheshire fell within the eastern territory of the Kingdom of Powys which may in fact have evolved out of the erstwhile canton – or CIVITAS – of the *Cornovii*: a strange turn of the circle.

Map (Figure 92)

- ● Settlement
- ○ Possible Settlement
- --- Roman Main Roads probably still in use

0   10   20   30miles

CARLISLE
SOUTHERN RHEGED
BURROW-IN-LONSDALE
MORECAMBE BAY
LANCASTER
RIBCHESTER
ELMET
WALTON-LE-DALE
WIGAN   MANCHESTER
Meols   Seteia
WARRINGTON
ANGLESEY   PRESTATYN
CAERHUN   ST. ASAPH   NORTHWICH   BUXTON
CAERNARFON   HOLT   CHESTER   MIDDLEWICH
Cair Segeint   BRYN-Y-GEFEILIAU   Cair Legion
Deva   Shavington
BANGOR-ON-DEE   Nantwich
TOMEN-Y-MUR   HOLDITCH
GWYNEDD   WHITCHURCH
CAER GAI   POWYS
BRITHDIR   WROXETER
WALL
PENKRIDGE

In this period, too, the Christian Church played an increasingly important role and we may see this in the legends surrounding men like Saint Germanus of Auxerre – provincial governor, soldier and bishop – and Saint Patrick; himself the product of a well-to-do Romano-British background. It may be that the Church in this region continued to be centred on Chester and, it must be said, Christian interest in the saltworks of central Cheshire may well have continued for at least another two hundred years, albeit under new regal control in Powys.

At Middlewich the picture is increasingly blurred; and it is difficult to sift and identify the archaeological evidence which may well be present. There are hints of some form of continuity, however, such as a sixth century brooch from the Shavington area. But, for the most part, we must rely on the likely implications of the few historical facts available to us. It is possible to build up something of a picture from them. We may imagine that the main roads continued to be used, although no longer maintained properly. The convergence of several of them on the Middlewich area must have continued to encourage traffic through what remained of the Roman settlement – but perhaps this was becoming a mixed blessing, for officialdom and not-always-friendly troops came with it. Nor were most of these roads of much more than local significance, although the

93 This long and straight stretch of Roman King Street is still a striking feature in the landscape to the north of Middlewich. The survival of this stretch indicates that it must have continued to be of regional importance for centuries after the end of Roman Britain.

KEY

 Fenland

 Cleared Heathland

 Open Woodland

 Dense Woodland

Roman Roads and pre-Roman tracks still in use

Rivers and streams

 Site of Roman fort

Ford

 English Buildings

Abandoned Roman settlement

Defended English Farmstead

Middlewich from the later seventh – early eighth centuries. The exact details of the processes and stages through which the Romano-British settlement came to an end remain unclear, but the beginnings of 'English' Middlewich were established in this period. This interpretation is based closely on archaeological discoveries and historical evidence from the area.

94 During the seventh century, central and western Cheshire fell gradually within the English Kingdom of Mercia. Although the old Roman roads had long since ceased to be looked after, they remained the principal, and only reliable, means of overland communication. Middlewich thus remained a place through which travellers [and armies?] passed. There was also the attraction of the valuable salt.

95 *(below right):* By the eighth century the remains of the former Roman settlement along King Street had long been abandoned and became increasingly derelict. In time, the more substantial and obvious remains became a convenient source of well-cut building-stone which was removed for reuse elsewhere in the area.

ones going westward, via Chester and Whitchurch, to the Powys heartlands, may have retained a long-distance importance.

As the venue for the celebrated *synod urb legion* [Synod at the City of the Legions] in the early seventh century, Chester – and hence probably the Middlewich area also – still lay within Celtic British territory; but the sand was running out. In 615, Aethelfrith of Northumbria fought and defeated Powys near Chester. Soon afterwards, Cheshire fell within 'English' territory. In the years that followed, what remained of the old Romano-British settlement ceased to exist; probably the community had been drifting away, back to its farming roots, for centuries. The buildings and roads, increasingly weed-strewn, gradually faded back into the landscape.

This was not an end but a new beginning. Life continued and, within the next century, English settlements would be established – outside the confines of the Roman site – near Kinderton Hall and in Newtonia, across the river. Both place-names are interesting: 'Kinderton' may be derived from CONDATE, in a form which the English thought they heard, and 'Newtonia' needs no translation as 'New Town'. Out of these, the Middlewich we know today would emerge: with new ways, new priorities, new politics, new economics but, for all that, something of the town's Roman heritage would come through.

96 *(far right):* The site of the Roman settlement at Middlewich in the later seventh – early eighth centuries. The Roman settlement has been completely abandoned, although the weed-covered humps and hollows betray its former existence along King Street. Instead, Mercian English settlements are developing at Kinderton and to the southwest of the crossings of the River Croco. The main Roman roads still continue to be used but, without regular maintenance, they are reverting to muddy tracks. Out of these new beginnings the Middlewich we know today is emerging.

ROADS: A ROMAN LEGACY

The most striking Roman features in the area today are stretches of the great roads which once converged on the Roman settlement. Given their former very considerable strategic importance it is somehow appropriate that the most obvious of these belong to the main road which once led from Wroxeter (VIROCONIUM), one-time legionary fortress and later cantonal capital city of the *Cornovii*, via Whitchurch (MEDIOLANUM) and Middlewich (CONDATE? SALINAE?), to the Mersey-crossing at Warrington. Their survival today indicates that they continued to be of some importance for centuries after the end of Roman Britain.

97 *(right):* The road from Wroxeter is preserved today in Sutton Lane, once an Iron Age track, upgraded in the first century AD as a great military artery and supply-route, and later becoming the main road to the Roman cantonal centre at Wroxeter.

98 *(far right):* The junction of Lewin Street with Sutton Lane reflects, to this day, the former junction of two great Roman roads in its vicinity: the road from Wall and Chesterton with the road from Wroxeter.

99 *(right):* 'New King Street' preserves the line of the Roman road northward from Middlewich to the crossing of the River Mersey at Warrington.

100 *(far right):* The line of the Roman road on King Street is preserved in the hedge and trees close to the entrance to Harbutt's Field.

101 *(right):* Looking north over the site of the Roman fort and saltworks at Middlewich in 1990. The Trent-Mersey Canal, Kinderton Street and the Town Bridge dominate the foreground. Harbutt's Field, the site of the newly discovered Roman fort, shows up clearly as a darker green field within the confluence of the Rivers Dane and Croco. Modern King Street meanders northward and crosses the railway immediately to the east of Harbutt's Field, before crossing the River Dane at Ravenscroft Bridge beyond. The Roman line of King Street is preserved clearly in 'New King Street' and the trees on the east side of Harbutt's Field. The approximate location of the Roman fort in Harbutt's Field is marked.

THE ROMAN MIDDLEWICH PROJECT

The Roman Middlewich Project was initiated in March 1999 to prepare a bid to the Heritage Lottery Fund for a project to promote the study, understanding and enjoyment of Roman Middlewich.

In August 2000 the application for Heritage Lottery Fund funding was successful and the Project was formally established.

The Project is a Partnership consisting of

Middlewich Town Council

Jonathan Williams
(Secretary)
The Town Clerk
Middlewich Council
Victoria Building
Lewin Street, Middlewich
Cheshire CW10 9AT

Tel: 01606 833434
Fax: 01606 836908
E-mail:
jonathan@jpawilliams.freeserve.co.uk
www.romanmiddlewich.co.uk

Congleton Borough Council

Harry Hopkinson
(Vice-Chairman)
Conservation and Design
Manager, 'Westfields'
Congleton Borough Council
Middlewich Road
Sandbach, Cheshire CW11 1HZ

Tel: 01270 769256
Fax: 01270 764829
E-mail: planning@congleton.gov.uk
www.congleton.gov.uk

Cheshire County Council

Adrian Tindall
(Chairman)
Principal Archaeologist
Environmental Planning
Cheshire County Council
Backford Hall, Backford
Chester, Cheshire CH1 6PZ

Tel: 01244 603160
Fax: 01244 603360
E-mail: tindalla@cheshire.gov.uk
www.cheshire.gov.uk

Gifford and Partners Limited

Tim Strickland
Director and
Chief Archaeologist
Gifford and Partners Ltd
20 Nicholas Street
Chester, Cheshire CH1 2NX

Tel: 01244 311855
Fax: 01244 314560
E-mail:
tim.strickland@gifford-consulting.co.uk
www.gifford-consulting.co.uk

Middlewich Heritage Society

Jane Weir
Middlewich Heritage
Society Representative
10 Yew Tree Close
The Orchards, Middlewich
Cheshire CW10 9QH

Tel: 01606 836336
Fax: 01606 836336
E-mail: janeweir@excite.co.uk

The Partners may be contacted for further information about the Roman Middlewich Project.

The Roman Middlewich Project Website is:
www.romanmiddlewich.co.uk

THE ACHIEVEMENTS OF THE ROMAN MIDDLEWICH PROJECT

The primary achievements of the Project have been to:

- produce an illustrated book on Roman Middlewich, suitable for the general reader and for schools.

- develop an education resource pack for use in the schools of Cheshire.

- set up a town trail with interpretation panels at key points in the town.

- create a new permanent exhibition on Roman Middlewich in the town library.

- produce a leaflet summarising the results achieved and designed to assist visitors to the town with directions to the town trail and exhibition.

- train a group of local people as town guides.

OTHER USEFUL CONTACTS

If you want other locally available information, general assistance or guidance round the town trail, the people and organisations to contact are set out below:

For information on the Salt Museum, which houses extensive Roman collections and displays on the salt-industry. Roman Middlewich Teaching Packs and Roman Cheshire Loans Boxes are also available from here:

The Manager
Cheshire Museums
The Salt Museum
162 London Road
Northwich
Cheshire CW9 8AB

Tel: 01606 41331
Fax: 01606 350420
E-Mail: jonesgl@cheshire.gov.uk

For information on the Heritage Trail:

Malcolm Thurston
10 Dorfold Close
Sandbach
Cheshire CW11 1EB

Tel: 01270 764695 (9am–5pm)
Fax: 01270 764062 (9am–5pm)
E-Mail: gatcraft@fsmail.net

For information on the Ermine Street Guard:

The Associate
Membership Secretary
10 Yew Tree Close
The Orchards
Middlewich
Cheshire CW10 9QH

Tel: 01606 836336 (9am–5pm)
Fax: 01606 836336 (9am–5pm)
E-Mail: janeweir@excite.co.uk

For information on the Middlewich Heritage Society:

The Secretary
16B Wheelock Street
Middlewich CW10 9AG

E-Mail:
jay.4.jennifer@netscapeonline.co.uk

For information on The Lion Saltworks – the only surviving open-pan saltworks in Britain:

The Project Manager
The Lion Saltworks
Ollershaw Lane
Marston
Northwich CW9 6ES

Tel: 01606 41823
Fax: 01606 41823
E:mail: afielding@saltworks.demon.co.uk
www.lionsaltwokrstrust.co.uk

Middlewich Library:

Library Manager
Lewin Street
Middlewich CW10 9AT

Tel: 01606 832801

Middlewich Information Centre:

Victoria Building
Lewin St
Middlewich CW10 9AT

Tel: 01606 832571
Fax: 01606 836908
Monday–Friday 9.00am–12.30pm
1.00pm–5.00pm

For more information further afield, the following organisations will be able to help.

For information on the Grosvenor Museum, which houses extensive displays and publications on the area in the Roman Period, especially Chester. Also for information on the Chester Walls and Amphitheatre:

Keeper of Archaeology
Grosvenor Museum
27 Grosvenor Street
Chester CH1 2DD

Tel: 01244 321616
E:mail: d.robinson@chestercc.gov.uk
www.chestercc.gov.uk

For information on the Archaeology of Chester and the surrounding area:

Chester City Archaeologist
Chester City Archaeology
27 Grosvenor Street
Chester CH1 2DD

Tel: 01244 321616
E:mail: m.morris@chestercc.gov.uk
www.chestercc.gov.uk

For information on Warrington Museum & Art Gallery, which houses displays of material from the Roman settlement at Wilderspool:

Curator
Warrington Museum
& Art Gallery
Bold Street
www.warrington.gov.uk/museum
Warrington WA1 1JG

Tel: 01925 442392
Fax: 01925 442399
E:mail: museum@warrington.gov.uk

For information on the Whitchurch Heritage Centre, which houses some spectacular finds from the Roman settlement at Whitchurch:

Jenny Surridge
Whitchurch Heritage Centre
12 St Mary's Street
Whitchurch
Shropshire SY13 1QY

Tel: 01948 665432 (Mon–Thus 9–5)
Fax: 01948 665432 (Fri 9–4.30, Sat 10–5)
Tourist info tel: 01948 664577
E:mail: whitchurch.heritage@care4free.net
www.shropshiretourism.com

For information on the Roman Site at Wroxeter:

English Heritage Site-
Museum at Wroxeter,
Wroxeter Roman Site
Wroxeter
Shropshire SY5 6PH

Tel: 01743 761330
Fax: 01743 761330
E:mail: wroxeter@english-heritage.org.uk
www.english-heritage.org.uk

For general information regarding places to go and stay in Cheshire:

Cheshire Tourism Office
Room 251
County Hall
Chester CH1 1SF

Tel: 01244 603107
Fax: 01244 603003
E:Mail: econdev@cheshire.gov.uk
www.cheshire.gov.uk

Council for British Archaeology (Northwestern Region):

The Secretary
39 Stalbridge Avenue
Liverpool L18 1HA

Tel: 0151 706 7814
E:mail: carolynek@career.u-net.com

Cheshire Sites and Monuments Record. The Cheshire County Sites and Monuments Record is available for consultation:

Dr Jill Collens
Environmental Planning
Cheshire County Council
Backford Hall
Chester CH1 6PZ

Tel: 01244 603204
E:mail: collensj@cheshire.gov.uk

Reconstruction of part of the defences of the Roman fort at Manchester:

Castlefield Roman Fort
Off Liverpool Road
Castlefield
Manchester

Tel: 0161 834 4026
E;Mail: enquiries@castlefield.org.uk
www.castlefield.co.uk

For information on the Chester Archaeological Society:

The Secretary
Ochr Cottage
Porch Lane
Hope Mountain
Caergwrle
Flintshire LL12 9HG

Tel: 01978 760834
E:mail: djpmason@dircon.co.uk

For information about discoveries and sites throughout Roman Britain:

The Association for
Roman Archaeology
75 York Road
Swindon
Wiltshire SN1 2JU

Tel: 01793 534008
www.zyworld.com/zarriba.ara.htm

SOME EVIDENCE FOR THE MIDDLEWICH ENVIRONMENT IN THE ROMAN PERIOD

Two samples of well-preserved organic material from Middlewich have been analysed. One from a Roman ditch adjacent to saltworks near King Street in 1969. Another from a Roman ditch at Kinderton Manor in 1997. This interesting exercise has identified a number of seeds from plants growing in the area. This has made it possible to draw some conclusions about the local environment in the Roman Period.

FROM SAMPLE ONE (1969) [Analysed in 2001]

          Cultivated oats   }
          Emmer and spelt-wheat   } both charred, with straw

And a number of weeds, some of them edible...

          Fat hen [grows on nutrient-rich ground, possibly land
which   has been fertilised with manure]

          Elderberry   }
          Raspberry   } all common on neglected overgrown
                                  areas such as woodland,
          Hemlock }   heathland and hedgerows

CONCLUSIONS

This looks like waste material from crop-processing. It could well have been used as fuel or tinder for brine-boiling. The oat seeds predominated and must have come from an important local crop.

Among the seeds was one example of coriander. This was a herb cultivated widely by the Romans. The Romans tell us that it was often used to add flavour to two staples of the Roman Army: porridge and mixed boiled greens. It was also used by the Romans to treat digestive disorders and for culinary purposes such as the flavouring and preservation of meat. At Middlewich it is also likely to have been mixed with salt as a meat-preservative.

FROM SAMPLE TWO (1997)

Buttercup, Stinging nettle, Hazelnut, Goosefoot, Fat-hen, Orache, Common chickweed, Redshank, Pale persicaria, Water-pepper, Knotgrass, Black bindweed, Dock, Radish, Coriander, Hemlock, Hogweed/parsnip, Hedge parsley, Bittersweet, Selfheal, Starwort, Thistle, Sow-Thistle, Water-plantain, Rush, Sedge.

CONCLUSIONS

Many of these seeds flourish on disturbed open waste-ground. Others flourish on nutrient- rich soils such as those used for livestock and also in cultivated fields or gardens. There is no evidence of cereal cultivation [but see Sample One]. More coriander was present [see Sample One also]. Some weeds are of the kind which flourish in slow-moving water such as that which might be present in waterlogged drainage-ditches.

TIMELINE

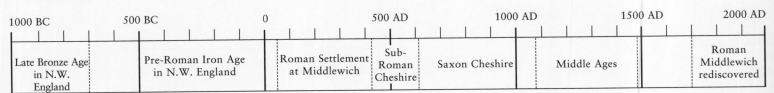

1000 BC	500 BC	0	500 AD	1000 AD	1500 AD	2000 AD
Late Bronze Age in N.W. England	Pre-Roman Iron Age in N.W. England	Roman Settlement at Middlewich	Sub-Roman Cheshire	Saxon Cheshire	Middle Ages	Roman Middlewich rediscovered

TABLE OF HISTORICAL EVENTS

A table of selected events in the history of Roman Middlewich
set in a wider Roman imperial context

Dates	Middlewich and surrounding area	Roman Britain	Roman World
BC 753			753. Rome founded
700 to 500	Farming settlements already well established in area.	End of Bronze Age culture and first beginnings of Iron Age in Northwestern Britain	
250 to 150	Trade up Mersey for Cheshire salt?	Traders from Mediterranean in Britain.	218–201. Hannibal in Italy.
146 73 58	Late Iron Age Cornovian settlements continue in Middlewich area.		146. Cathage destroyed. 73. Spartacus slave revolt. 58. Julius Caesar in Gaul.
55/4 44		55/4. Caesar in Britain.	44. Caesar assassinated.
27 **AD** 14 33 40	Salt-production and trade continues.	40. Death of Cunobelinus.	27. Augustus proclaimed. 14. Death of Augustus. 33. Crucifixion of Jesus Christ.
41			41. Accession of Claudius.
43		43. Romans invade Britain.	
47–50	Roman soldiers active in the area.	47-50. Romans v Caratacus.	
50/1	Roman soldiers pass through Middlewich en-route for the Mersey.	50/51. Defeat of Caratacus. Cartimandua hands him over to Rome.	
54			54. Death of Claudius, accession of Nero.
57	Roman soldiers march through Middlewich?	57. Romans support Cartimandua v Venutius.	
58/59/60	Roman soldiers in Cheshire.	58/59. Romans in Wales.	
60/61	60/61. Rebellion of Boudica.		
68			68. Death of Nero.
69	Roman soldiers active in Middlewich area. Auxiliary fort?	69. Trouble in Brigantia. Cartimandua overthrown.	69. Civil War. Accession of Vespasian.
70		70. Romans invade Brigantia.	70. Jewish War.

Dates	Middlewich and surrounding area	Roman Britain	Roman World
71–4	Agricola and a large Roman force march through Middlewich. Fort at Harbutt's Field.	71–74. Roman campaigns in Brigantia.	
74–7		74-77. Romans in N. Wales. Chester under construction.	
77–9	New road from Chester, via Northwich to Manchester, avoids Middlewich. Supplies from Middlewich continue via Wilderspool?	77–79. Agricola advances into Scotland.	79. Death of Vespasian. Accession of Titus. Colosseum finished. Vesuvius destroys Pompeii.
			81. Death of Titus. Accession of Domitian.
80–84		80–84. Roman Army in Scotland.	
84		84. Agricola recalled to Rome.	
c.86–96	Expansion of military saltworks at Middlewich. ALA CLASSIANA in residence?	86–90. Romans withdraw from Scotland.	
105	Middlewich diploma granted.		
105–117	Development of military saltworks continues.	Army consolidates hold on Tyne-Solway region. Chester rebuilt in stone.	98–117. Reign of Trajan. Empire expands to greatest extent.
117			117. Death of Trajan. Accession of Hadrian.
122	Hadrian visits Wroxeter and passes through Middlewich?	122. Hadrian visits Britain. Construction starts on Hadrian's Wall.	
132	Army departs from Middlewich?	Some troops withdrawn.	132. Jewish War.
c.138–c. 150	Beginnings of civilian saltworks.	Roman Army in Scotland. Construction of Antonine Wall.	138. Death of Hadrian. Accession of Antoninus Pius.
161	Trade with northern garrisons.		161. Death of Antoninus Pius. Accession of Marcus Aurelius.
175	Middlewich saltworks continue to develop. (some ironsmithing, copperworking and leatherworking also).	Continued warfare in the North.	Wars on the Danube.
180			180. Death of Marcus Aurelius. Accession of Commodus.
192			192. Commodus murdered.
193			193. Accession of Septimius Severus.
195	Some troops removed from Chester	195. Clodius Albinus and troops from Britain v Septimius Severus.	
197	Middlewich not far south of new provincial border.	Britain subdivided into two smaller provinces.	Septimius Severus defeats Albinus at Lyons.

Dates	Middlewich and surrounding area	Roman Britain	Roman World
208–11	Salt production continues to develop at Middlewich.	Septimius Severus and family campaigning in Britain. Severus dies at York.	
c.211	Middlewich flourishing		Caracalla returns to Rome. Constitutio Antoniniana – all freeborn in Empire now Roman citizens.
250's–280's	Beginnings of decline at Middlewich.	Pirates on East and West coasts.	Army reorganised.
284			284. Accession of Diocletian.
286	Pirates in Mersey Basin and Dee Estuary	Carausius, usurper, in Britain and Gaul.	
293			293. Empire divided into two.
296		Constantius Chlorus in Britain.	
306	Middlewich in BRITANNIA PRIMA	Picts invade Britain. Constantius and son, Constantine, return. Constantius dies at York. Britain subdivided into four.	Constantine proclaimed emperor.
306–350	Saltworking continues on a reduced scale at Middlewich. Lead salt-pans in widespread use. Some salt-works in area under control of Christian community (Bishop Viventius of Chester?)	Coastal defences improved.	Christianity now the religion of the Roman State.
383	Last regular Roman soldiers withdrawn from Chester?	Magnus Maximus leaves Britain with troops in bid for empire.	
395			395. Accession of Honorius.
410	Some saltworking alongside small farming community continues.	Rescript of Honorius. Local Authorities now to fend for themselves.	Goths sack Rome.
454			454. Attila the Hun in Italy.
476	Sub-Roman Celtic British Kingdoms.	Emergence of Saxon Kingdoms.	476. Romulus Augustulus, last Emperor of the West, deposed. End of Western Empire.
601	Synod at Chester. Middlewich still in British territory.	St Augustine's mission to the English.	
615	Middlewich in English territory.	Aethelfrith of Northumbria wins Battle of Chester.	
By 650	Roman settlement gradually abandoned. English settlements in area.		

THE PRINCIPAL ARCHAEOLOGICAL DISCOVERIES RELATING TO EACH OF THE PERIODS DESCRIBED IN THIS BOOK.

Compare these maps and lists of discoveries with the maps and aerial views in each chapter. It will be possible to see how and why the evidence can be used to build up a picture of life in Middlewich at different dates throughout the Roman period and after the arrival of the Anglo-Saxons in the seventh century.

MIDDLEWICH BEFORE THE ROMANS

LIST OF ARCHAEOLOGICAL DISCOVERIES

[The numbers refer to numbers on the map. They show where each discovery was made].

8 A cast bronze terret-ring. Late Iron Age.
11 A cast bronze scabbard-chape. Late Iron Age.
65 2000. Bronze terret-ring.
74 1964–9. J.D.Bestwick's excavations adjacent to 57 King Street. Late pre-Roman Iron Age pottery, circular timber building.
78 1969–72. J.D.Bestwick's excavation at Kinderton Street. Pre-Roman Iron Age pottery, circular timber building.
79 1972–4. J.D.Bestwick's excavation. Pre-Roman Iron Age pottery.
84 1998–9. Archaeological watching-brief by Gifford and Partners on land off King Street, on the southern edge of, and to the south of Harbutt's Field: Pre-Roman Iron Age pottery, circular timber building.
88 1999. Archaeological watching-brief by Gifford and Partners on land at Kinderton Hall Farm. Pre-Roman field-system.
93 1820–66. Mr. B.Vawdrey collected finds in and around his property at Kinderton Old Hall during excavations for a pond and drainage-ditches.
121 Historically marshy area. Possibly the location of early brine-springs exploited in the Iron Age and Roman periods.
122 Probable prehistoric trackways.
124 Aerial photograph indicating possible Iron-Age buildings/features.

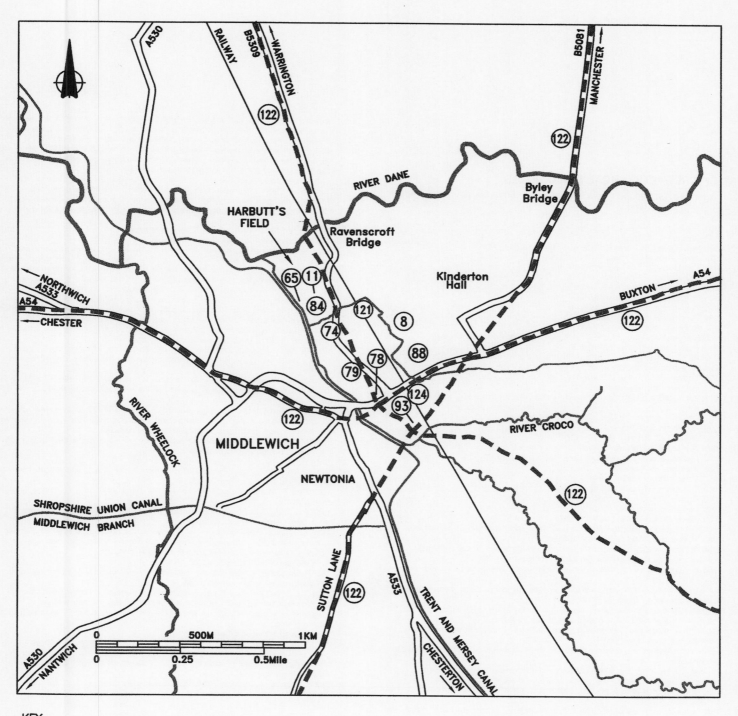

A530

RAILWAY

B5309

WARRINGTON

122

B5081

MANCHESTER

122

RIVER DANE

Byley Bridge

HARBUTT'S FIELD

Ravenscroft Bridge

Kinderton Hall

NORTHWICH A533

A54

CHESTER

65 11

84

121

8

74

78

88

79

BUXTON

A54

122

RIVER WHEELOCK

124

93

RIVER CROCO

122

MIDDLEWICH

NEWTONIA

SHROPSHIRE UNION CANAL
MIDDLEWICH BRANCH

SUTTON LANE

A533

122

TRENT AND MERSEY CANAL

CHESTERTON

122

| 0 | 500M | 1KM |
| 0 | 0.25 | 0.5Mile |

A530

NANTWICH

KEY

▬ ▬ ▬   Pre—Roman tracks

THE ROMAN ARMY AT MIDDLEWICH C.AD 48–C.130

LIST OF ARCHAEOLOGICAL DISCOVERIES

[The numbers refer to numbers on the map. They show where each discovery was made].

20 1998. Roman coin of Vespasian (AD 69–79).
24 1998. Roman coin of Augustus (7–6 BC).
27 1998. Romano-British bronze 'bow' brooch (late first century AD).
31 1998. Roman coin of the Republic (147 BC).
34 1998. Roman coin of the Republic (47–46 BC).
37 1998. Roman coin of Trajan (AD 98–117).
38 1998. Roman coin of Trajan (AD 98–117).
39 1998. Roman coin of Vespasian (AD 69–79).
40 1998. Roman coin of Trajan (AD 98–117).
41 1998. Roman coin of the Republic (87 BC).
42 1998. Roman coin of Trajan (AD 98–117).
44 1998. Romano-British bronze 'bow' brooch (late first/early second century AD).
45 1998. Roman coin of Trajan (AD 98–117).
47 1998. Romano-British bronze 'bow' brooch (late first/early second century AD).
51 1999. Roman pottery and coins (first to second century AD).
52 1999. Roman coin of Trajan (AD 112–114).
53 1999. Roman coin of Vespasian (AD 71).
54 1997. Earthworks Archaeological Services Excavation at Kinderton Hall. (military-style ditch, leather sandal, human cremation-burial (?) and pottery of first and second century AD).
56 1939. Roman bronze military diploma (AD 105).
57 1999. Roman coin of Trajan (AD 98–117).
61 2000. Romano-British bronze 'bow' brooch (late first century AD).
62 2000. Romano-British bronze 'bow' brooch (late first century AD).
65 2000. Romano-British bronze 'bow' brooch.
66 2000. Roman coin of Trajan (AD 98–117).
67 2000. Roman coin of Trajan (AD 98–117).
68 2000. Romano-British bronze 'bow' brooch.
69 2000. Roman coin of the Republic (123 BC).
71 2000. Roman coin of Trajan (AD 98–99).
72 2000. Romano-British bronze 'trumpet' brooch (late first to early second century AD).
73 1960. Harding and Blake's excavation. (pottery).
74 1964–9. J.D.Bestwick's excavations adjacent to 57 King Street. (timber buildings, leatherworking, pottery of the first and second centuries AD).
75 1964–9. J.D.Bestwick's excavation.. (timber buildings and pottery of the second century AD).
76 1964–9. J.D.Bestwick's excavation at 22 King Street. (timber buildings, camp stool and pottery of the second century AD).
77 1969. J.D.Bestwick's excavation at Dane Street. (timber buildings, cobbled street and pottery wasters of the late first to early second century AD).
78 1969–72. J.D.Bestwick's excavation at Kinderton Street. (timber buildings and pottery of the first and second centuries AD).
79 1972–4. J.D.Bestwick's excavation. (timber buildings, ditches and pottery of the first and second centuries AD).
80 1972–4. J.D.Bestwick's excavation at Poolhead Farm. (timber buildings, brine-pit, briquetage, oven, ditch and pottery of the late first and second centuries AD).
81 1993. Archaeological watching-brief by Gifford and Partners at Lewin Street. (road surface, ditch, pottery).
82 1993–4. Archaeological evaluation by Gifford and Partners at Harbutt's Field. (geophysical plot of Roman fort, ditches, timber buildings and pottery).

84 1998–9. Archaeological watching-brief by Gifford and Partners on land off King Street, to the south of Harbutt's Field. (Road, timber buildings, clay floors, pits, ovens, briquetage, chimney-pot, bronze brooches and pottery of the first and second centuries AD).
85 1998–9. Archaeological watching-brief by Gifford and Partners on land off King Street, to the east of Harbutt's Field. (Road, timber buildings, clay floors, pit, briquetage, bronze brooch and pottery of the first and second centuries AD).
88 1999. Archaeological watching-brief by Gifford and Partners on land at Kinderton Hall Farm. (Road, ditches, brine-pits, briquetage and pottery of the second century AD).
89 2000. Archaeological evaluation by Gifford and Partners on land off King Street. (Road, ditches, timber buildings, clay floors, briquetage and pottery of the first and second centuries AD).
90 1995. Archaeological excavation by Gifford and Partners on land at Kinderton Hall Farm. (Field boundary ditches, quernstone and pottery).
91 1849–50. Archdeacon Wood traced the line of the Roman road known as King Street across Harbutt's Field to a fording-point on the River Dane just to the west of Ravenscroft Bridge, also identifying Harbutt's Field as the site of a Roman camp. (coins and pottery).
92 1820–66. Mr. B. Vawdrey collected Roman finds during the diversion of King Street to cross the railway at Ravenscroft bridge. (flue-tile, pottery, coins and quernstones).
93 1820–66. Mr. B. Vawdrey collected Roman finds in and around his property at Kinderton Old Hall during excavations for a pond and drainage ditches. (cremation urn, road surface, timber lined shafts, floor tile, pottery, coins, briquetage, leather sandal and quernstones).
94 1820–66. Mr. B. Vawdrey collected Roman finds in and around the site of the saltworks on King Street. (pottery, coins and quernstones).
95 1820–66. Mr. S. Pickering recorded the line of a Roman road to the north of the gasworks off King Street, during excavations for gravel extraction on the eastern side of fields 35 and 36.
96 1820–66. Mr. B. Vawdrey collected Roman finds to the north of Poolhead Farm during the excavation of drainage trenches associated with the mill pond. (pottery including amphorae).
97 1854. During excavations for the construction of a gasometer Roman finds were collected, though believed to have been redeposited from the construction of the Trent and Mersey canal. (briquetage, quernstones, bronze objects and pottery).
98 1820–66. Mr. B. Vawdrey collected a Roman rotary quern during building demolition on the National School site off Lewin Street.
102 1998. Roman coin of Trajan (AD 98–117).
105 1920–2. Mr. S. Pickering collected 23 Roman coins from Fields 35 and 36 (dated first century BC to the second century AD).
106 1922. Prof. D. Atkinson's excavation. (clay floors, slag, pottery of the first and second century AD).
109 1972. J.D.Bestwick located a ditch indicating the western boundary of the settlement, which contained first century AD pottery.
110 1962–5. Various excavations by F. H. Thompson, D. Stubbs and J.D.Bestwick. (Timber buildings, pebble floors, road-side ditches, pottery of late first and early second century, including a rotary quern, roof tile and a Roman coin of Nerva).
114 1989. Roman coin of the Republic (89–88 BC).
115 1936. During extension-works to playing-fields off Wheelock Street, 12 complete samian vessels were uncovered from a sandpit.
116 1989. Mr. E.Waddelove made observations during construction work at Church Fields which he interpreted as part of a possible Roman fort. (ditch and pebble surface).
117 1996. Archaeological evaluation by Manchester University at Church Fields failed to locate Roman finds on this site.
118 Roman camp in Harbutt's Field.
119 1970. Roman pottery found by Mr. A. Earl of 59 King Street during extension work in his garden.
121 Historically marshy area. Possibly the location of early brine-springs exploited in the Iron Age and Roman periods.
122 Probable prehistoric trackways (still in use in Roman Period).
123 Roman roads (certain and possible).

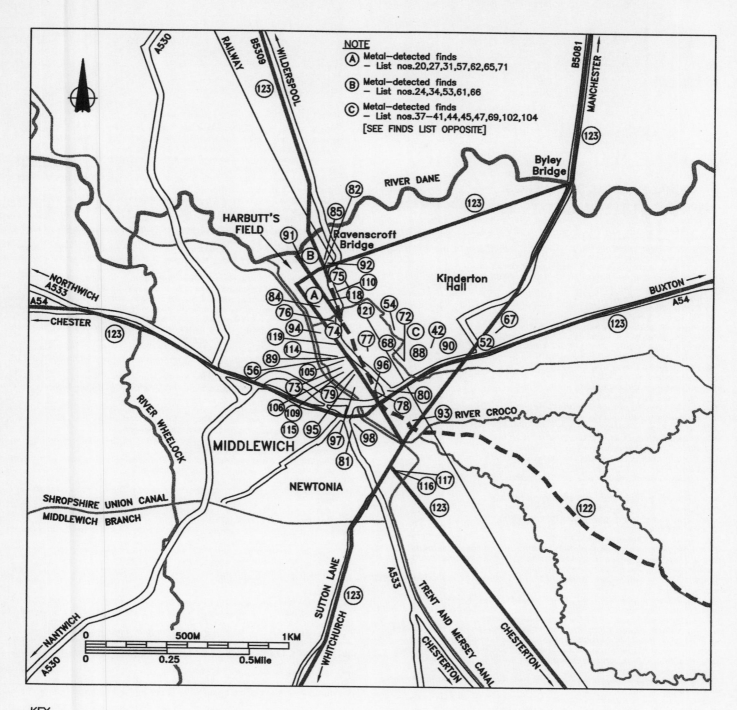

NOTE

Ⓐ Metal-detected finds
— List nos.20,27,31,57,62,65,71

Ⓑ Metal-detected finds
— List nos.24,34,53,61,66

Ⓒ Metal-detected finds
— List nos.37—41,44,45,47,69,102,104
[SEE FINDS LIST OPPOSITE]

KEY

▬ ▬ ▬ Pre—Roman tracks still in use

▬▬▬▬ Roman roads (certain and possible)

ROMAN MIDDLEWICH
C.AD 130–C.260

LIST OF ARCHAEOLOGICAL DISCOVERIES

[The numbers refer to numbers on the map. They show where each discovery was made].

19 1998. Roman pottery found at 55 King Street.

22 1998. Roman gilded bronze finger-ring.

23 1998. Romano-British bronze brooch (second century AD).

25 1998. Romano-British bronze 'trumpet' brooch (second century AD).

26 1998. Romano-British bronze 'trumpet' brooch (second century AD).

28 1998. Romano-British bronze slide key.

29 1998. Romano-British bronze key handle.

30 1998. Romano-British bronze 'disc' brooch/harness fitting.

32 1998. Roman coin of Hadrian (AD 132).

33 1998. Roman coin of Marcus Aurelius (AD 161–176).

35 1998. Romano-British bronze 'trumpet' brooch (second century AD).

36 1998. Romano-British bronze 'trumpet' brooch (second century AD).

46 1998. Roman coin of Antoninus Pius(AD 138–161).

48 1998. Romano-British bronze fitting.

49 1998. Roman coin of Hadrian (AD 117–138).

50 1998. Roman coin of Hadrian (AD 131).

51 1999. Roman pottery and coins (first to second century AD).

53 1999. Roman coin of Antoninus Pius (AD 141).

54 1997. Earthworks Archaeological Services excavation at Kinderton Hall. (cobbled track, timber building, oven, briquetage and pottery of second century AD).

55 1998. Roman silver coin-hoard, probably buried some years after c. AD 125.

57 1999. Roman coin of Marcus Aurelius (AD 161–176).

58 1999. Romano-British bronze brooches, a bronze hair-pin and a coin of Hadrian (AD 117–138).

59 2000. Romano-British bronze brooches, a bronze seal-box lid, a lid steelyard weight and pottery.

60 2000. Romano-British bronze brooches and a lead lamp-holder.

63 2000. Romano-British bronze 'trumpet' brooch (second century AD).

64 2000. Romano-British bronze 'plate' brooch (second century AD)

65 2000. Romano-British iron key.

70 2000. Roman coin of Antoninus Pius(AD 141).

73 1960. Harding and Blake's excavation. (timber buildings, a brine-kiln, briquetage, pottery).

74 1964–9. J.D.Bestwick's excavations adjacent to 57 King Street. (timber buildings, brine-pits, yard surfaces, brine-kilns, briquetage, gold finger ring).

75 1964–9. J.D.Bestwick's excavation. (timber buildings and pottery of the mid-late second century AD).

76 1964–9. J.D.Bestwick's excavation at 22 King Street. (timber buildings and pottery of the second century AD).

77 1969. J.D.Bestwick's excavation at Dane Street. (timber buildings).

78 1969–72. J.D.Bestwick's excavation at Kinderton Street. (timber buildings, floor surfaces, brine-kilns, briquetage, timber revetted ditch/leat, pottery of second to third centuries).

79 1972–4. J.D.Bestwick's excavation. (timber buildings, ditches, iron-smithing and pottery).

80 1972–4. J.D.Bestwick's excavation at Poolhead Farm. (timber buildings, brine-pit, briquetage, oven, ditch and pottery).

81 1993. Archaeological watching-brief by Gifford and Partners at Lewin Street. (road surface, ditch, pottery).

82 1993–4. Archaeological evaluation by Gifford and Partners at Harbutt's Field. (Evidence of abandoned Roman fort, ditches, timber buildings and pottery).

84 1998–9. Archaeological watching-brief by Gifford and Partners on land off King Street, to the south of Harbutt's Field. (Road, timber buildings, clay floors, pits, ovens, briquetage, chimney-pot, bronze brooches and pottery of second and third centuries AD).

85 1998–9. Archaeological watching-brief by Gifford and Partners on land off King Street, to the east of Harbutt's Field. (Road, timber buildings, clay floors, pit, briquetage, bronze brooch and pottery of the second and third centuries AD).

87 1997. Archaeological evaluation by Gifford and Partners at 20 Lewin Street. (pottery)

88 1999. Archaeological watching-brief by Gifford and Partners on land at Kinderton Hall Farm. (Road, ditches, brine-pits, briquetage, cremation-urn, iron snaffle-bit and pottery of the second to third centuries AD).

89 2000. Archaeological evaluation by Gifford and Partners on land off King Street. (Road, ditches, timber buildings, clay floors, briquetage and pottery of the second and third centuries AD).

90 1995. Archaeological excavation by Gifford and Partners on land at Kinderton Hall Farm. (Field boundary ditches, quernstone, and pottery).

91 1849–50. Archdeacon Wood traced the line of the Roman road known as King Street across Harbutt's Field to a fording-point on the River Dane just to the west of Ravenscroft Bridge. (Coins and pottery).

92 1820–66. Mr. B. Vawdrey collected Roman finds during the diversion of King Street to cross the railway at Ravenscroft bridge. (flue tile, pottery, coins and quernstones).

93 1820–66. Mr. B. Vawdrey collected Roman finds in and around his property at Kinderton Old Hall during excavations for a pond and drainage ditches. (cremation urn, road surface, timber-lined shafts, floor tile, pottery, coins, briquetage, leather sandal and quernstones).

94 1820–66. Mr. B. Vawdrey collected Roman finds in and around the site of the Salt Works on King Street. (pottery, coins and quernstones).

95 1820–66. Mr. S. Pickering recorded the line of a Roman road to the north of the Gasworks off King Street, during excavations for gravel-extraction on the eastern side of Fields 35 and 36.

96 1820–66. Mr. B. Vawdrey collected Roman finds to the north of Poolhead Farm during the excavation of drainage-trenches associated with the mill-pond. (pottery including amphorae).

97 1854. During excavations for the construction of a gasometer Roman finds were collected, though believed to have been redeposited from the construction of the Trent and Mersey canal. (briquetage, quernstones, bronze objects and pottery).

98 1820–66. Mr. B. Vawdrey collected a Roman rotary-quern during building demolition on the National School site off Lewin Street.

99 1820–66. Mr. B. Vawdrey noted large quantities of dressed building-stone were present in field 43, to the east of King Street, during ploughing.

100 Early nineteenth century. Mr. B. Vawdrey reported the finding of stone foundations to a [supposed Roman] building on the Newtonia side of the River Croco, opposite Harbutt's Field.

103 1980. Romano-British bronze 'trumpet' brooch (second century AD).

104 1984. Roman coin of Hadrian (AD 117–138).

105 1920–2. Mr. S. Pickering collected 23 Roman coins from fields 35 and 36 (some dated to the third century AD).

106 1922. Prof. D. Atkinson's excavation. (clay floors, slag, pottery of the second and third centuries AD and a Roman coin of Hostilianus AD 250–1).

107 1965. Dr. G. Webster found Roman pottery during the excavation of a drainage-trench.

108 1949. Second century AD pottery found during the excavation of a cutting for a garage entrance.

110 1962–5. Various excavations by F. H. Thompson, D. Stubbs and J.D.Bestwick. (Timber buildings, pebble floors, road-side ditches, pottery of late second century, a rotary quern, roof tile).

111 1969. J.D.Bestwick's excavation at 22 King Street. (timber buildings, folding camp-stool and pottery of the second century AD).

113 1980. Mr. K. Lawrence found a Roman coin of Antoninus Pius and a Romano-British bronze key head.

115 1936. During extension-works to playing-fields off Wheelock Street, 12 complete samian vessels were uncovered from a sandpit.

119 1970. Roman pottery found by Mr. A. Earl of 59 King Street during extension work in his garden.

121 Historically marshy area. Possibly the location of brine-springs exploited in the Roman period.

122 Probably prehistoric trackway (still in use in Roman Period).

123 Roman roads (certain and probable).

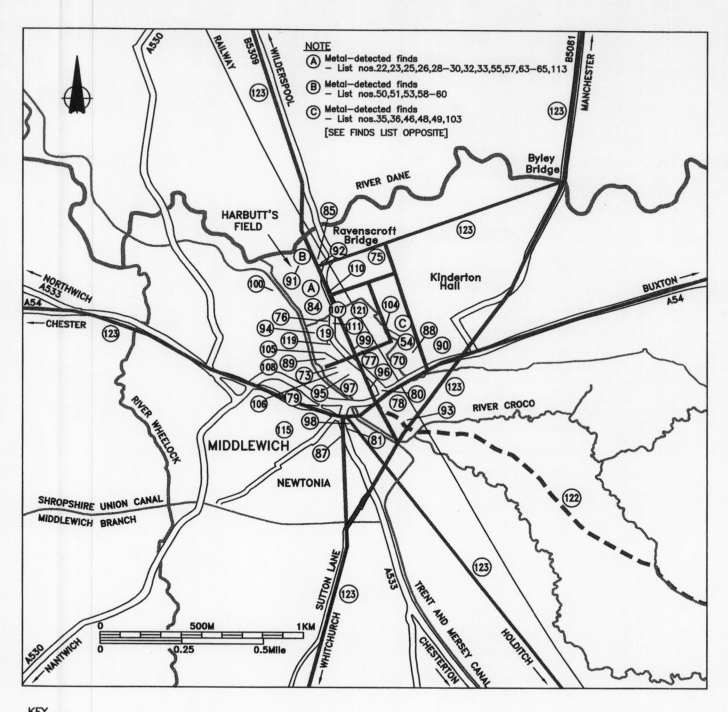

LATE ROMAN MIDDLEWICH

LIST OF ARCHAEOLOGICAL DISCOVERIES

[The numbers refer to numbers on the map. They show where each discovery was made].

21   1998. Roman coin of Constantine I (AD 306–337).

43   1998. Roman coin of Tetricus I (AD 271–3).

74   1964–9. J.D.Bestwick's excavations adjacent to 57 King Street. (timber buildings, brine-pits, yard surfaces, brine-kilns, briquetage, gold finger ring, pottery of the fourth century AD).

78   1969–72. J.D.Bestwick's excavation at Kinderton Street. (timber buildings, floor surfaces, brine-kilns, briquetage, timber revetted ditch/leat, iron shears and pottery of the fourth century AD).

79   1972–4. J.D.Bestwick's excavation. (timber buildings, ditches, iron-smithing and pottery of the fourth century AD).

80   1972–4. J.D.Bestwick's excavation at Poolhead Farm. (timber buildings, brine-pit, briquetage, oven, ditch and pottery of the fourth century AD).

81   1993. Archaeological watching-brief by Gifford and Partners at Lewin Street. (road surface, ditch, pottery).

86   2000. Archaeological excavation by Gifford and Partners at Lewin Street. (pottery).

89   2000. Archaeological evaluation by Gifford and Partners on land off King Street. (Road, ditches, oval timber buildings, clay floors, briquetage and pottery of the fourth century AD).

90   1995. Archaeological excavation by Gifford and Partners on land at Kinderton Hall Farm. (Lead salt-pan and pottery).

91   1849–50. Archdeacon Wood traced the line of the Roman road known as King Street across Harbutt's Field to a fording-point on the River Dane just to the west of Ravenscroft Bridge. (Coins and pottery).

101   1997. Four fragments of an inscribed Roman lead salt-pan, bearing the cast inscription LVTAMI (meaning 'belonging to Lutamus').

112   1971. D.Stubbs reported finds of lead salt-pans during excavations for the pumping station.

121   Historically marshy area. Possibly the location of brine-springs exploited in the Roman period.

122   Probable prehistoric track (still in use).

123   Roman roads (certain and possible).

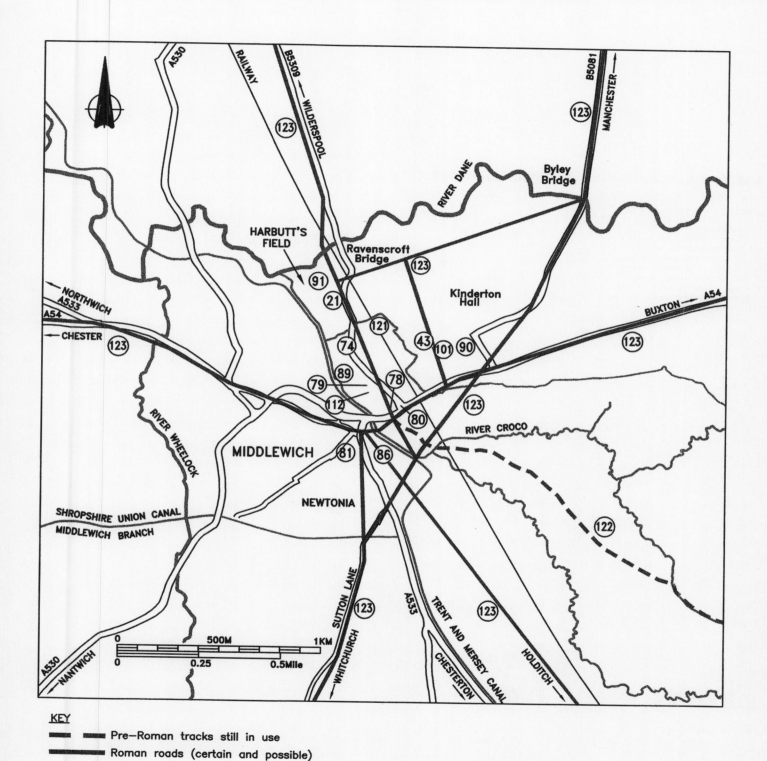

KEY

▬▬ ▬▬ Pre—Roman tracks still in use

▬▬▬ Roman roads (certain and possible)

AFTER THE ROMANS

A SELECTION OF ANGLO-SAXON FINDS FROM MIDDLEWICH

[The numbers refer to numbers on the map. They show where each discovery was made].

12 Kinderton Hall manor.
13 Croxton manor.
14 Cast bronze stirrup.
15 Cast bronze strap-end.
16 Cast bronze strap-end.
17 Silver penny of Aethelred II.
18 Anglo-Saxon dress-pin.
122 Possible prehistoric track still in use in the Saxon Period.
123 Roman roads still in use in the Saxon Period.

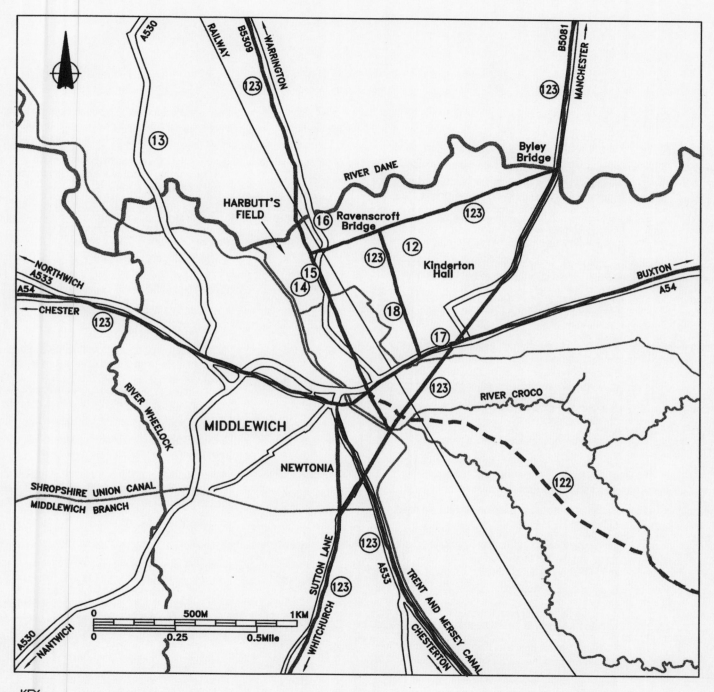

KEY

━ ━ ━ Pre—Roman tracks still in use

━━━━━ Roman roads still in use

EXPLANATION OF SOME TERMS USED IN THIS BOOK

Adiutrix: Roughly translated as 'additional' or 'reserve'; title given to the Second Legion raised by the Emperor Vespasian in c.70 and posted to Chester soon afterwards.

Ala [plural = *alae*] Translated as 'wing'. A term used to describe the cavalry regiments of the Roman Army.

Amphora: [plural = *amphorae*] Large storage jar, often used to transport commodities such as olive oil and wine.

Antiquarian: A student or collector of antiquities. A term often used to describe the earliest amateur archaeologists.

Auxiliary Regiment: Military unit raised from recently conquered or subject peoples for service in the Roman Army. The term Auxiliary is also sometimes used to describe an individual soldier from such a unit.

Barrow: A mound of earth piled up over a grave to create a monument.

Bow Brooch: Roman brooch shaped like a bow.

Brine: Groundwater with high salt content rising to the surface in either natural springs or specially constructed wells.

Brine-boiling: Process of heating brine in order to extract salt from it.

Brine-kiln: Term used to describe the structure of salt-pans set over a fire or furnace designed for brine-boiling prior to the extraction of salt.

Brine-spring: Point at which brine comes to the surface.

Briquetage: Term used to describe roughly made fired clay objects used in salt-production.

Cairn: A mound of stones piled up to commemorate an event, provide a landmark or as a tomb.

Canton: Tribal territory formally reconstituted into an area or region administered by a local or regional government authority. Called a *civitas* by the Romans.

Constitutio Antoniniana: Law enacted in the early third century elevating all freeborn people of the Roman Empire to the status of Roman citizen.

Cremation-burial: Burial, often in an earthenware pot or urn, of the fragmentary remains of a body which has been consumed by fire.

Dalmatia: Approximately modern Croatia

Denarius: [plural = *denarii*] Roman silver coin. Standard unit of pay for Roman soldiers.

Diploma: A formal grant of Roman Citizenship in the form of two inscribed bronze sheets. Often given to auxiliary soldiers on retirement.

Disc Brooch: Flat, circular brooch with pin at rear.

Edict: A government order.

English: Term used to describe the people of Germanic descent who began to settle in Britain and gradually replaced the Romano-British in later Roman times, and afterwards often referred to as 'Anglo-Saxons'.

Evaluation: The clarification and identification of the archaeological potential of a site, often by means of carefully located trial-trenches.

Flue-tile: A tile specially made to provide a hot-air duct, usually in a Roman under-floor heating system or bath-house.

Fosse: A defensive ditch or trench.

Foundation-Trench: Trench dug to accommodate the foundations of a wall.

Geophysical Survey: Survey carried out to assess the potential of a site without the need for excavation. Such survey may include measurement of electrical and magnetic anomalies in the soil. Ground-penetrating radar, seismic soundings and metal-detection are sometimes used in support. The results may be substantiated by trial-excavation.

Germanic immigration: Term used here to describe the processes and movements whereby people of German descent settled in the western provinces of the Roman Empire. This used to be called 'the barbarian invasions'. The Germans today refer to this as 'the wanderings of the peoples'.

Graffito: A message scratched or painted on a wall or other surface such as the side of an *amphora*.

Gratuity: Grant of money to a Roman Soldier on his retirement from service.

Holding-tank: Clay, wood or wicker-lined tank designed to hold or collect brine prior to its removal for boiling.

Iron Age: Term used to describe the last few hundred years BC in Britain, when iron was in widespread use.

Knobkerrie: A wooden club.

Legion: A division of nearly 6000 Roman citizen-soldiers.

Legionary: A soldier belonging to a Roman Legion.

Marching-camp: Temporary fortified camp used for short stops by Roman troops on the march.

Mortarium: [plural = mortaria] A grinding bowl.

Pastoral-farming: Simple livestock farming in open pastures.

Picts: In the late Roman period this was increasingly the term used to describe the peoples north of Hadrian's Wall, especially in parts of Scotland.

Plate Brooch: Flat brooch, often of diamond or rectangular shape, with pin at rear.

Purple: The colour associated with Roman Emperors and the high aristocracy. The phrase 'to vie for the purple' thus refers to an attempt to become emperor.

Repair-and-maintenance: Term used to describe the regular, even daily, programme of maintaining a fort and its infrastructure in good serviceable condition.

Romano-British: Term used to describe the people of Britain during the Roman occupation.

Rotary quern: A quernstone, often made of hard basalt, designed for grinding corn into flour by means of a circular motion or rotation.

Round-house: A circular house with conical thatched roof.

Salt-pan: Pan made of either briquetage or lead in which salt residue is collected by boiling brine.

Scabbard-chape: The carved or moulded metal end to a scabbard.

Scots: Tribes from central Ireland who emigrated to Scotland in and after the late Roman period and who gave their name to that country.

Seal Box: A small box, often of bronze, attached to a document, and designed to hold and protect a wax seal impression from accidental damage or wear.

Sept: Subdivision or smaller unit of a large tribe.

Slide Key: Roman key designed for a lock with a sliding mechanism.

Slag: Vitreous refuse or waste material from the smelting of iron or copper ore.

Snaffle bit: A plain and simple bit forming part of the bridle of a horse.

Subsistence farming: Small scale agriculture, sufficient to provide people with the basic necessities.

Tanning: Process of soaking raw hides in tannic acid whereby they are converted into leather suitable for use in manmade articles such as shoes, belts, tents and so forth.

Terret-ring: Ring on a harness through which reins are passed.

Timber-Frame: An arrangement of timbers set up to provide a frame for a wall or partition. The spaces between the timbers are usually infilled with other material ranging from clay, wattle and daub to brick.

Trumpet Brooch: Distinctive brooch rather like a large ornamental safety-pin.

Unguent: Sweet smelling oil or ointment.

Watching-brief: Term used to describe an arrangement in which an archaeologist keeps watch on new construction work, in order to record rapidly any archaeological finds or features which may appear briefly.

A SELECTION OF BOOKS FOR FURTHER READING

ROMAN BRITAIN IN GENERAL

Birley, A., *The People of Roman Britain.* Batsford, 1988.

Breeze, D.J., *The Northern Frontiers of Roman Britain.* Batsford, 1982.

Creighton, J., *Iron Age Coins.* Cambridge University Press, 2001.

Cunliffe, B., *Iron Age Communities in Britain.* Book Club Associates, third Edition 1991.

Esmonde Cleary, A.S., *The Ending of Roman Britain.* Batsford, 1989.

Frere, S, S., *Britannia: a history of Roman Britain.* Revised edition, Routledge and Kegan Paul, 1987.

Hanson, W. S., *Agricola and the Conquest of the North.* Batsford, 1987.

Higham, N., *Rome, Britain and the Anglo-Saxons.* Seaby, 1992.

Hurst, J. D., *Savouring the Past: The Droitwich Salt Industry.* Hereford and Worcester, 1992.

Ireland, S., *Roman Britain – a sourcebook.* Croom Helm, 1986.

Johnson, A., *Roman Forts.* A and C Black, 1983.

Jones, G. D. B. and Mattingly, D., *An Atlas of Roman Britain.* Guild Publishing, 1990.

Margary, I. D., *Roman Roads of Britain*, Third Edition, 1973.

Peddie, J., *The Roman War Machine.* Alan Sutton, 1994.

Salway, P., *Roman Britain.* Oxford University Press, 1981.

Salway, P., *The Oxford Illustrated History of Roman Britain.* Oxford University Press, 1981.

Strong, D. and Brown, D., *Roman Crafts.* Duckworth, 1976.

Wacher, J., *The Towns of Roman Britain.* Batsford, 1974.

Webster, G., *The Roman Invasion of Britain.* Book Club Associates, 1981.

Webster, G., *The Roman Imperial Army.* Revised Edition, A and C Black 1985.

ROMAN CHESHIRE AND SURROUNDING AREA

Bullock, J. D., *Pre-Conquest Cheshire 383-1066.* Cheshire Community Council, 1972.

Carrington, P., *Chester*, Batsford, 1994.

Carrington, P. (Eds)., *'Where Deva Spreads her Wizard Stream'*, Chester Occasional Papers, 3, Chester City Council, 1996.

Carrington, P. (Eds)., *'From Flints to Flower Pots'*, Chester Occasional Papers, 2, Chester City Council, 1994

Cowell, R. W. and Philpott, R. A., *Prehistoric, Romano-British and Medieval Settlement in Lowland Northwest England.* National Museums and Galleries on Merseyside, 2000.

Curzon, J.B., *CONDATE CASTELLUM, The rediscovery of the Roman Site on Castle Hill in Northwich*, Vale Royal Borough Council, 2000.

Curzon, J.B., *'Paying for the Invasion'*, Cheshire History, 40, 2000-2001.

Harding, J. and Johnston, R., *Northern Pasts, Interpretations of the Later Prehistory of Northern England and Southern Scotland*, BAR, 302, 2000.

Hartley, B and Fitts, L., *The Brigantes.* Alan Sutton, 1988.

Higham, N. J., *The Origins of Cheshire..* Manchester University Press, 1993.

Higham, N. J., T*he Kingdom of Northumbria: AD 350-1100.* Alan Sutton, 1993.

Nevell, M. (Eds)., *'Living on the Edge of Empire'*, Archaeology North West, 3 (Issue 13), CBA North West, 1999.

Petch, D. F., *'The Roman Period'*, in Victoria History of Cheshire. I, London, 1987.

Petch, D. F., *Roman Salt Making*, Cheshire Libraries and Museums leaflet.

Shotter, D. C. A., *'The Roman Conquest of the North-west,'* Transactions of the Cumberland and Westmorland Antiquarian and Archaeological Society. C, 2000.

Robinson, D. J., *'The Romans and Ireland again'*, Journal of the Chester Archaeological Society. 75, 1998-9.

Shotter, D. C. A., *Romans and Britons in North-west England*. University of Lancaster, Second Edition, 1997.

Shotter, D. C. A., *Roman Coins from North-west England*. Centre for North West Regional Studies, 2000.

Strickland, T. J., *Roman Chester* in Victoria History of Cheshire V, London, 1995.

Strickland, T. J., *Roman Chester,* Hendon Publishing, 1992.

Strickland, T. J., *Romans at Wilderspool,* Greenalls, 1995.

Thacker, A. T., *'Anglo-Saxon Cheshire'*, in Victoria History of Cheshire I, London, 1987.

Thompson Watkin, W., *Roman Cheshire*. Reprinted with new Introduction by D. F Petch, E P Publishing Ltd., 1974.

Thompson, F. H., *Roman Cheshire*. Cheshire Community Council, 1965.

Webster, G., *The Cornovii*. Revised edition, Alan Sutton, 1991.

Webster, G., *Boudica*. Revised edition, Batsford, 1993.

Webster, G., *Rome against Caratacus*. Revised edition, Batsford, 1993.

ROMAN MIDDLEWICH

Nevell, M. D., 'SALINAE, Roman Middlewich. A Review of its development,' in *Cheshire History,* 27, 1991.

Pearson, E., *Environmental Remains from Middlewich,* Site I, Cheshire. Worcestershire County Council, 2001.

Thompson Watkin, W., 'KINDERTON (CONDATE)' in *Roman Cheshire*. Reprinted edition, 1974, 243-251.

Petch, D. F., 'Middlewich' in *Victoria History of Cheshire,* I, London, 1987.

Shotter, D. C. A., 'Middlewich, the evidence of coin-loss', *Journal of the Chester Archaeological Society,* 75, (1998-9), 2000, 51-60.

Penney, S. and Shotter, D.C.A., 'An Inscribed Salt-pan from Shavington, Cheshire', *Britannia*, XXVII, 1996, 360-365.

Penny, S., 'An Inscribed Salt-pan from Middlewich', *Archaeology Northwest*, 4 (issue 14), 1999.

Bestwick, J. D., 'Romano-British Inland Salting in Middlewich (SALINAE), Cheshire, in Salt, *The Study of an Ancient Industry, Colchester,* 1975.

Thompson, F. H., 'Middlewich', in *Roman Cheshire,* 1965, 91–97.

In addition to these a great deal of important and relevant information is to be found in the *Transactions of the Historical Society of Lancashire and Cheshire*, the *Journal of the Chester Archaeological Society*, *Britannia* (the Journal of the Society for the Promotion of Roman Studies), *The Past Uncovered* (Newsletter of Chester Archaeology), *Archaeology Northwest* (Bulletin of Council for British Archaeology, Northwest region). In addition, a number of otherwise unpublished reports are lodged with the Cheshire County Sites and Monuments Record.

AUTHOR'S ACKNOWLEDGEMENTS

In addition to those mentioned in the Preface, thanks are also due to many others who have been associated with this book and with the Roman Middlewich Project. Simon Warburton, Chris Johnson and Ian Marshall for many of the photographs.

Jeffersons Air Photography for the aerial photographs of Middlewich, used as a basis for the painted aerial views.

Donald and Elsie Brown, Peter Cox, Ben Hart, Dorothy Hughes, Joy Leathwood, Mary Morris, Julie Smalley, Malcolm Thurston, Geoffrey Williams, Jonathan Williams and Alan Wrench, the Middlewich town guides on whom the lengthy training-programme was inflicted, as book-writing progressed.

Jill Collens, for assistance with the County Sites and Monuments Record, for the photograph of the gold coin from Warmingham and for the aerial photograph of King Street.

Anthony Martin for much support in the office which has freed me to devote some attention to writing this book.

Tim Morgan, for a number of high quality drawings of artefacts which have been the basis of some of the reconstruction paintings.

Frances Richards, for information on coriander.

Dan Robinson, Keeper of Archaeology at the Grosvenor Museum, for considerable help with access to the diploma and other finds from Middlewich and for the translation of the diploma text.

Ian Smith, for information about some of the animals in the area during the Roman Period.

David Shotter, for assistance with the interpretation of the significance of the Roman coins from Middlewich.

Don Stubbs, for much assistance with the finds made in Middlewich during the 1960s and 1970s.

Peter Moore-Dutton, for providing access to the finds made by Benjamin Vawdrey, his ancestor, now at Tushingham Hall.

Rob Philpott and Ron Cowell for help in understanding Cheshire before the Romans.

Rosemary Mullen for help and advice concerning the educational aspects of the book.

Stephen Penney and Nick Herepath for much help with the tracking-down and interpretation of the significance of many Roman finds from Middlewich.

Middlewich Heritage Society, especially George Twigg and Alan Earl.

Members of the Vale Royal Metal Detecting Society – in particular Tom Wallace and Nigel Townley,

Crewe and Nantwich Metal Detecting Society – in particular Howard Lehepuu, Kevin Guest and Geoff Dickinson; and the Rolls Royce Historical Artefacts Association – David Stubbs and David Kitchen, for readily providing information on many Roman finds from the Middlewich area.

His Excellency, Luigi Amaduzzi, Italian Ambassador to the Court of St James, for his interest in the project.

Mr Marcello Cavalcaselle, Italian Consul, also for his interest and for kindly agreeing to launch the Middlewich Festival.

My good friends John and Helen Tweed, for providing me with the ideal location for writing.

Discoveries in August 2001

At the time of going to print, a major developer-funded archaeological excavation was carried out to the west of King Street, some 300 metres south of the Roman fort discovered recently in Harbutt's Field. Discoveries included further spectacular evidence of timber-framed buildings in the saltworking ribbon-development on King Street, with narrow properties sloping down to the River Croco, at the rear. Further examples of well-preserved plank-lined and wicker-lined brine-shafts, wells and holding-tanks were found, together with two east-west roads or streets. [See particularly the illustration of this part of the settlement on page 36, the saltworking scene on page 37 and the Aerial View on page 39 for an appreciation of these and other related discoveries].